Instructions for using AR

LET AUGMENTED REALITY CHANGE HOW YOU READ A BOOK

With your smartphone, iPad or tablet you can use the **Hasmark AR** app to invoke the augmented reality experience to literally read outside the book.

1. Download the **Hasmark app** from the **Apple App Store** or **Google Play**

2. Open and select the (vue) option

3. Point your lens at the full image with the and enjoy the augmented reality experience.

Go ahead and try it right now with the Hasmark Publishing International logo.

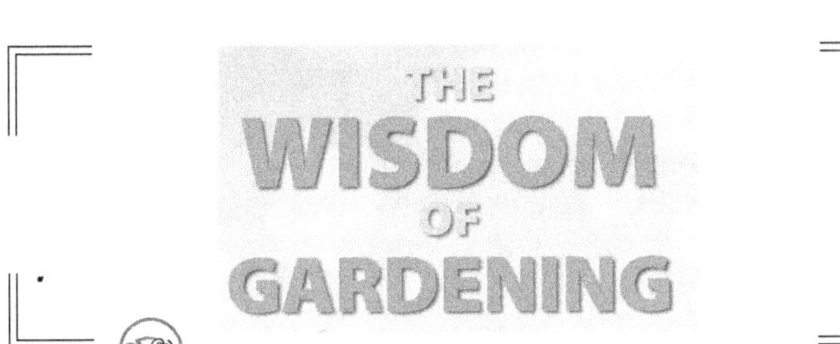

ENDORSEMENTS

"David has certainly had over thirty years of practical experience, to write *The Wisdom of Gardening*. There is a wealth of information and humour in the book and I am getting a lot from it. I always like instructional books like this, with old and new tricks and techniques. Many people, new to gardening will also get a lot out of it."

—Jane Edmanson OAM
Horticulturalist, author, radio and TV host
(Gardening Australia)

(Jane has an Honorary Life Membership of the Horticultural Media Association of Victoria (2013) for outstanding service to horticulture and the media. She has received the Gold Laurel and Hall of Fame Award by Horticultural Media Association Australia and the Golden Wattle Award by the Australian Institute of Horticulture. Jane is a very prominent Australian horticulturalist, author, TV, and radio personality. She has been with the weekly TV program *Gardening Australia* since its beginning in 1990, as a founding presenter.)

"The book is so notable in its approach. Enjoy this book. It's funny, enlightening, and imbued with a profound knowledge of gardening."

—Alan Hollensen
B. Ed., M. Ed. TESOL, M.A.
(See Foreword)

"This book has a good balance between humorous and down-to-earth practical advice. I liked the format of short sharp observations, tips, and hints. It is certainly going to help lots of gardeners, old and new to enjoy their garden."

—Jennifer Stackhouse
BA. (Hons.) Fine Arts

(Jennifer Stackhouse is a horticulturalist, author, and garden writer. She has edited *Australia Horticulture* magazine and *Burke's Backyard* magazine as well as *ABC Gardening Australia* magazine. She has written many books including *Garden*, which won a Book Laurel in 2013. She currently edits *Greenworld* magazine and writes for the Saturday magazine in the *Mercury* newspaper in Hobart, Tasmania.)

THE WISDOM OF GARDENING

David Grodski

Hasmark Publishing
www.hasmarkpublishing.com

Editor: Harshita Sharma harshita@hasmarkpublishing.com
Cover Design: Anne Karklins anne@hasmarkpublishing.com
Illustrator: Ellie Abrat Udvary
Book Design: Amit Dey amit@hasmarkpublishing.com

ISBN 13: 978-1-77482-121-3
ISBN 10: 1774821214

DEDICATION

*This book is dedicated to Jean,
my mother-in-law, and Leon, my father.
They both taught me a lot about gardening, but
more importantly, about life.*

"To plant a garden is to believe in tomorrow."

—Audrey Hepburn

CONTENTS

FOREWORD

"During my 16 years working for the Nursery and Garden Industry Association of Victoria, the state's peak body for ornamental horticulture, I had the pleasure of meeting many interesting people. These were growers, retailers, and people working in the allied trades, but one of the most interesting was David Grodski.

David had trained as a medical doctor and retrained in landscape design.

He and his wife Helen ran a small, but delightful retail nursery in Brighton, Melbourne and the nursery served as a shop window for his landscaping business.

David brought to his business and his interactions with customers, a deep and abiding love of plants and gardening, a sense of whimsy, and a dedication to the highest standards of professional endeavour; it was quite a combination. His customers loved him for it, his industry peers appreciated him for it, and now via his book, a wider audience can gain access to this amazing combination of qualities.

My own professional interactions with David and his impressive staff at The Gardeners Corner Store nursery took place over the course of about a decade.

Certainly, long enough to form a deep appreciation of his approach, not just to plants and gardening, but more importantly to people. This appeared to be the guiding light in what he did; plants were important, but people were more important.

This book, so notable in its approach, so blessed with insight and humour, is yet another example of David's deep concern for people, that they thrive as their gardens thrive, that if you like, they grow as their gardens grow and that they enjoy themselves doing it.

Gardening is a pleasure, and David reminds us of that on every page.

Enjoy this book. It's funny, enlightening, and imbued with a profound knowledge of gardening, but also a deep knowledge and appreciation of gardeners – of you and me."

—Alan Hollensen
B. Ed., M. Ed. TESOL, M.A.

ABOUT THE AUTHOR

Doctor David Grodski is a retired medical practitioner, a retired horticulturalist and landscape designer, a world bestselling author, and a proud Rotarian for over thirty-seven years.

His first book, *The Wisdom of Wellness (WOW)*, became an international best seller when judged by Amazon in June 2020. It was voted number one in holistic medicine in France, Canada, the USA, and Australia.

David decided to write his first book about his own vision of wellness and life, and what steps and choices one could take to have wellness. As 20/20 means perfect vision, he felt qualified to give this advice in 2020, as he had just reached "the age of wisdom", turning seventy-five years old and at the same time, celebrating fifty years of his marriage. These milestones, he hoped, had given him enough wisdom to write a book that gave practical advice on twenty topics, which showed everyone how to be at their best, at all times.

His love of horticulture emerged when his father bought a small farm and gave it to his children in the hilly Dandenongs, on the outskirts of Melbourne. This gesture gave David and his siblings a chance to connect with nature and share a weekend retreat with their children and friends. Besides learning how to care for Angus steers, David also learnt a lot about horticulture (planting, pruning, watering, and feeding) as well as practical agricultural skills like fence building, handling farm equipment, making concrete, and property management. These basic landscaping skills gave David an advantage in his future horticultural career.

Although David did not study Latin, his knowledge and understanding of plants came from the Latin he learnt as a medical undergraduate, especially with the study of botany. David gained insight into the meaning and the origin of plant names, which often indicated where each plant came from and where it should be planted in a garden.

More importantly, medicine taught David the importance of having good communication skills, problem-solving skills, caring skills, integrity, reliability, and the ability to find creative outcomes in complicated situations. David attributes these latter skills to his ultimate success in horticulture.

After being in the medical career for almost twenty years, he joined The Gardeners Corner Store nursery in Bayside, Melbourne, which was started by him and his wife in 1988.

A career in horticulture led to teaching practical gardening skills to students at Prahran TAFE for a few years, but he stopped after facing the reality of working those additional hours.

After five years in the industry, David studied landscape technology at Burnley Horticultural College, Melbourne with inspirational tutors like Andrew Laidlaw, John Patrick, and James Hitchmough, to name a few. His studies covered all aspects of design, selection of plants, landscaping techniques, and the analysis of all the parameters of weather.

In addition to working in the nursery, he found time to work with his landscaping team. They all created every style of garden, from a three-square-metre memorial garden at the back of a church, to large-scale domestic gardens requiring concept plans, master plans, construction plans, and planting plans.

To have some fun, the landscape team also displayed their diversity at many International Flower and Garden shows at the Carlton Gardens, Melbourne. These were quirky and theatrical gardens that always had a message. For example, "The Box family of Box Hill", where the message was, "The family that gardens together stays together".

Here, different sized topiary English box plants (Buxus sempervirens) were dressed up in clothes, with artificial heads, arms, and legs attached, tools in hand, "gardening" together.

The nursery, with its landscaping business, went on to win the state industries' top awards, sponsored by Yates consecutively for three years, from 2004 to 2006. Alan Hollensen from the NGIV was a great mentor for the business and the industry and David is indebted to him for his encouragement. These awards had an enormous reassuring impact on the whole team and business, knowing that one's peers had recognised and acknowledged all of their effort, three years in a row.

At the same time, the horticultural industry was brought to its knees with the impact of Stage 4A water restrictions, following devastating years of drought. The business subsequently shut down, but reopened six weeks later, on a different site. Key staff (John Parish and Cathryn McEwen) were invited to become equal partners, and all continued at the new Gardeners Corner Store for another ten years. That property was sold to developers recently, so David then retired from horticulture.

The good news is that the business survives today in East Brighton, Melbourne, being run by Catherine McEwen and Tim Bouma. Nothing has changed, as the "Store" is still offering the same high standard of plants, ornamental pieces for the house and garden, nursery products, and the highest level of service. An *Online Plants Melbourne* website continues as well, the website showing some pot plants hanging on a clothesline by pegs.

Final Thought

*"The lesson I have thoroughly learnt,
and wish to pass onto others, is to
know the enduring happiness that the
love of a garden brings."*

—Gertrude Jekyll

Note: "A <u>horticulturalist</u> is an expert in or student of garden cultivation and management". (Oxford Dictionary)

ABOUT THE BOOK

David's motivation to write this book followed a thirty-year career in all matters horticultural. Running a prize-winning horticultural business meant that all staff had to constantly be at their best and be prepared to learn new skills every day. This enabled everyone to work smarter, quicker, and easier than their competitors. Having the nursery gave everyone involved a better knowledge of plants and access to the best quality plants, often at a reduced price. This knowledge combined with what they saw each day in the many gardens (old and new), enabled all of them to readily visualise what had worked well and what had failed. In essence, each garden was a "classroom", where one could learn so much.

As Betsy Garmon said, "My garden is my favourite teacher".

At that time, it was unusual for a nursery owner to also work on "tools", but this gave the landscape business a great advantage, as it took the "intellectual property" of the nursery into people's homes.

After all this hands-on experience, it was now time for David to share his knowledge widely. The research for the book started when David reviewed his large selection of gardening books, as well as those in his local library. It soon became apparent that there were many books with beautiful pictures of plants and gardens, and others with some useful technical advice. Interestingly, there were very few books that gave great PRACTICAL ADVICE. Only one book by Shirley Stackhouse, *The Gardening Year*, mentioned something simple, such as applying sunscreen and wearing a hat whilst gardening. This book was one of the few books that gave garden advice, specifically for Australian gardens, as most gardening books available at the time were English or American. We at the Gardeners Corner Store nursery sold hundreds of copies, as we believed this book was the best of its kind for local conditions. So, if you ever find an old copy, buy it.

David had never seen any gardening book with an abundance of practical advice, from advising one to take a bottle of water to drink whilst gardening (as you would with other strenuous activities), or something as simple as washing one's hands at the end of the day.

This lack of useful and practical tips and tricks forms the basis of David's book, and he is now comfortable in sharing these in a very simple way.

This book reminds David of the excitement one may experience if one found one's grandfather's or grandmother's gardening journal in their garden shed, assumed lost for years.

David's book is now available to all existing gardeners, to improve their skill levels, and to any potential gardeners who would like to get their hands dirty. It is filled with over seven hundred **"tricks, tips, hints, crafty procedures, and pieces of advice"**. These have been collected and used over the years, and all can enhance one's gardening experiences.

Each *"tip and trick"* has a *"Final Thought"* that offers a *quote*, a quirky piece of advice, or a little humour. Sometimes there is an anecdotal comment close by.

At the end of the day, gardening should be rewarding and enjoyable, so let's get started and have some fun.

Final Thought

"The love of a garden is a seed once sown, never dies."

—Gertrude Jekyll

INTRODUCTION

Creating and maintaining a garden requires immense knowledge. The task always seems to be formidable and sometimes creates a feeling of inadequacy and possible disinterest.

When I was young, it was not uncommon to have a grandparent living in a bungalow, in the rear garden. This grandparent taught their family how to grow this or that, how to repair things, and perhaps preserve fruit and vegetables. Before grandparents moved away (often due to their daughters entering the workforce), career mothers did most of the gardening, sharing plants, cuttings, and ideas with other career mothers (or "Domestic Goddesses", as the famous international chef, Nigella Lawson, called them). Men generally did the lawns and any heavier work at home. This "army" of home gardeners passed on their knowledge, believing that gardening was a rewarding family pursuit. In recent years, gardening pursuits have been impacted by social changes as houses have become larger and hence, gardens smaller.

The popularity of units and apartments has also limited the scope for gardening. Gone are the days when a home was perfectly placed on its block, with adequate outdoor space, where the family spent a lot more time at home on the weekends and often outside.

Also, in years gone by, commercial distractions did not exist, as only churches, petrol stations, and nurseries were open on the weekends, which meant that people mainly stayed at home, often to garden. Now every store, cinema, and sporting venue is open all weekend, and the opportunity to garden has to compete with these distracting choices. The age of "Consumerism" has taken over.

As a result, our busier lifestyles don't allow any realistic opportunity to meet Mother Nature, face to face.

We now need to get a "crush" on gardening and not be "crushed" by it.

I am hoping my book can revive the gardening secrets (tips and tricks) that my parents and grandparents taught me.

Final Thought

"A garden that is not worth a little trouble is not worth anything."

—Wayne Winterwood

TIPS AND TRICKS
(Essential Advice for the Keen Gardener)

THE BENEFITS OF GARDENING

Not everyone can imagine many benefits of gardening, but after they read the list of positive benefits below, they may change their minds. I hope so.

For many, gardening involves getting dirty, hot, and sweaty, and cursing the ever re-emergence of weeds that will never grow in straight lines. They see their other leisure options being eroded by a task that they often find boring.

My tips and tricks

Fortunately, gardening is an activity that

- offers regular exercise.
- is performed in the fresh air.
- can be performed in the sunshine with the obvious Vitamin D benefits.
- can be very creative.
- gives a sense of productivity.
- offers a sense of responsibility.
- can have a calming effect on the mind.
- can provide a healthier diet.
- can be done with other family members, creating the advantages of a "team approach".
- creates excess fresh and seasonal fruit, vegetables, herbs, and flowers to share with family, friends, and neighbours.
- makes one pleasantly tired, so that one can sleep more peacefully.
- connects us with nature and therefore gives our lives balance.
- creates a sense of community, as it fosters human connection.
- teaches us how to handle tools and equipment and work creatively with our hands.

Final Thought

"The glory of gardening, hands in the dirt, head in the sun, and your heart with nature, where you don't just nurture the body, but your soul as well."

—Alfred Austin

HOME CONTENTS (odds and sods) THAT MAY BE USEFUL OUTSIDE

There are many bits and pieces, or "odds and sods" (things that are usually small and unimportant) in every household that may have some practical use in your garden. You may not have recognised any of them, but you will be surprised by the following list.

My tips and tricks

- Use an old photo album to store plant labels for future reference.
- Prior to gardening, scrape your nails in household soap, so that they are easier to clean after gardening is completed.

- Apply a barrier cream to your hands, which also makes them a lot easier to clean at the end of the day.

- Use a magnifying glass to help identify bugs.

- An old tape measure can be very useful in the garden.

- Use candle wax to seal a tree wound after pruning.

- Cut old pantyhose into strips, for use as garden ties, especially for tomatoes.

- Find an unused diary, as it makes an ideal journal to record pest treatments, feeding regimes, and planting dates, for example. You can also record rainfall and temperature details if these parameters are important to you.

- Use a permanent marking pen for labelling.

- Household chalk has lots of uses. Chalk can be used to mark out the game of hopscotch, mark a measurement on the ground, or temporarily colour a tree trunk for a party.

- Take vegetable scraps outside, to be put into the compost bin.

- Make your own homemade "kitchen liquid fertiliser". Vegetable scraps (offcuts) can be put into a large pot of water and boiled for an hour. When cool, this homemade liquid fertiliser can be poured into pot plants or onto the garden.

- Cut plastic milk bottles into strips for plant labels.

- Old plastic bottles can also be cut up for a tree guard (when the top and bottom of the bottle are removed). Just split open the remaining bottle and fit this new tree guard around the trunk, at ground level.

- Old plastic bottles can also be made into a scoop or converted into little protective surrounds for seedlings.

- Wash an old, unused mop head and use it as a source of garden ties.

- Recycled polystyrene boxes can be broken into small pieces and placed as "crock" in large pots to lighten their weight. At the same time, you save money, not having to buy that extra potting mix.

- Recycled cans or plastic bottles can be used in the same way.

- Old gumboots can have their "foot" cut off and then be used as a shield for one's forearm when pruning very thorny plants.

- Disused cardboard boxes are very useful. When flattened, they can be used to smother weeds. To stop them flying away, just place enough soil on them, and eight weeks later, you will find that the weeds have died.

- A flattened box can also be used to shield a plant, whilst spraying another.

- Find a cardboard box the same height as a small hedge that you want to clip. Just move the box along with your foot, to give you the desired height to clip the hedge, and see if you can land most of the clippings in the box. Try this, as it really works and saves you time when cleaning up.

- Old newspapers can also be used for smothering weeds, and if torn up, can be added to the compost bin. Shredded newspaper can be soaked in fertiliser and placed in furrows in your vegetable garden.

- Water used to boil vegetables or hard-boiled eggs can be saved and when cool, it can be poured onto the garden as liquid fertiliser, instead of being thrown down the sink.

- Used coffee filter papers can be placed inside the base of a pot to prevent soil from falling out through the drainage hole, and to prevent bugs from crawling back in.

- Used coffee grounds can be added to the garden as a source of nitrogen, phosphorus, magnesium, potassium, and copper.

- Used tea bags can be added to the compost bin or added to cold water to make a weak brew that can be poured over your pot plants. Some gardeners believe tea bags are beneficial when placed around azaleas. Just cover them with a little soil for a more aesthetic look.

- Try this simple but effective weedkiller: Vinegar (Apple Cider) can be used at the recommended dose of one part water to one part vinegar, which can then be sprayed onto the weeds.

- Cut aluminium foil into strips or keep used aluminium pie dishes. These can then be attached to trees, and as they flap around, they act as deterrents to birds and possums.

- Keep your eggshells as they can be ground up and then added to the garden. They are a great source of calcium, especially for roses.

- Add old copper coins into the soil around tomato plants as they help prevent tomato blight (a fungal disease). Just bury them to a depth of ten centimetres.

- Bring out the beer, as it makes a great snail and slug killer. Just a small amount is needed. You can have the rest.

- Turn a struggling azalea or gardenia into a thriving plant by adding any cola drink, which is slightly acidic. One hundred millilitres per plant is enough, and then water it in.

- Banana peels, especially when chopped up, can add potassium to roses and tomatoes.

- Old woollen blankets or clothes, when cut up, can make interesting hanging basket liners that retain moisture readily.

- A few teaspoons of baking soda around tomatoes reduces acidity. Therefore, your tomatoes will be sweeter.

- Soluble aspirin has the same salicylic acid as growth hormone and will help revive a struggling indoor plant. One tablet dissolved in water every couple of weeks is enough to do the trick until the plant is better.

- Old bananas, when hung in slow ripening tomato plants, help out by releasing ethylene.

- An old toothbrush dipped in pest oil is a great way to treat white scale on older rose bushes, and at the same time, it physically removes the dead scale.

- Unused plastic shower caps (collected from hotel stays) are ideal as new plant covers.

- Washed, unsoiled nappies or cut-up kitchen sponges (Wettex) can be added to hanging baskets or pots to help retain moisture.

- Ash from your fireplace can be sprinkled lightly around roses or added to the compost heap. It is rich in calcium, potassium, and magnesium. If placed around perennials that snails and slugs love (like hosta species), the gritty ash will stop them from sliding over.

- The drawers of an old chest can be used as a miniature herb or succulent container.

- Unused plastic chopsticks can be used as plant markers.

- Old wire coat hangers can be straightened out and used for plant supports or as a spike when cooking marshmallows.

- Glad wrap (plastic wrap) can be used to seal in moisture when doing aerial cuttings on branches. These cuttings are small wounds on a branch, which are then surrounded by sphagnum moss and tied to the branch. This is then covered with plastic wrap.

- Place a raw egg under a new plant to provide it with essential nutrients. Our grandparents liked this idea as they did not have access to modern fertilisers. They only had compost as the major source of nutrients for their garden and if lucky, some animal dung from a rural relative. Personally, I prefer my eggs soft boiled.

- Cinnamon can be used as an antifungal when sprinkled onto seedlings or sprayed onto affected plants.

- Lint from your clothes dryer can be added to hanging baskets to help retain moisture.

- Vacuum cleaner fluff is high in human and pet hair, skin flakes, and mites and is worth burying around tomato plants or adding to the compost.

- Lint can also be packed into empty toilet rolls, which can then be used for seed planting. When ready, just plant it all in the garden.

- Fish tank water is best poured onto the garden than down the sink.

- Plastic shopping bags make great shoe protectors when gardening, or as a cover over a paint tray when painting outside.

- Clear nail polish can be used on plant labels so that the signage lasts longer.

- Any soot you have can be mixed with water as a super boost nutrient for sweet pea flowers (Lathyrus odoratus).

- Silicone gel can be used to assist climbers on a wall in preference to plugs and screws. Just place a blob every metre or so as the creeper grows.

- Tomato juice mixed with dog food (at a ratio of one and a half tablespoons per meal) may help neutralise the chemical in dogs' urine that burns the lawn.

- Empty baked bean cans can be cleaned, painted with bright colours, and then drilled with multiple holes. These can then be hung on trees with a small candle inside. A dramatic outcome.

- Small pieces of household soap can be broken up and dissolved in water. This makes an environmentally multipurpose bug spray.

- Large tins can have their base pierced multiple times and become ideal spreaders of lawn seed and fertiliser.

- A large tarpaulin (when laid flat) can easily help collect clippings and therefore save time cleaning up, smother areas of weeds, or assist in moving heavy objects along the ground.

- A small fold-up seat can be useful when it is time to have a break.

- Honey can be used as a rooting compound when preparing cuttings for future plants.

- Blu-Tack or sticky tape is useful for helping self-clinging climbers get started.

- Cellophane tape wrapped around your hand is a great way to remove aphids. Stabilise the affected branch and then use the taped hand to collect the aphids, sticky side out.

- Old hot water bottles can be used outside as kneeling pads, as can old pillows placed inside a sturdy plastic bag.

- Zip ties are very strong and can be used to help attach climbers to their frame or to help establish the framework for espaliering fruit trees.

- Unused lead-free house paint can be used as a wound dressing after pruning.

- Old pieces of carpet or underlay can be ideal for smothering weeds. Cut into pieces for easy use, one by two metres. A small square of old carpet can be placed on your compost bin to help it retain moisture.

- Unused cutlery can create an interesting wind chime, using different lengths of fishing lines.

I am not suggesting you make use of all the tips and tricks mentioned above, but I am sure that even if you only choose five items, you should feel very proud of yourself.

15

Final Thought

*"When we finally go outside,
let me show you my garden, a
friend you can visit anytime."*

HEALTH AND SAFETY ISSUES WHEN GARDENING

Whilst health and safety issues are of paramount importance and are enforced in the workplace, the same issues at home appear to have less prominence or adherence. Accidents may happen in the garden, but most are preventable.

My tips and tricks

- Always wear a mask when spraying chemicals and fertilisers.

- Always use the recommended dose when spraying.

- Always wash out spraying equipment after use.

- Wear gloves, especially when pruning roses.

- Never use fingers (as often recommended) to firm in potting mix or check soil moisture. You can't tell if something sharp is in the soil or whether there are nasty fungal spores that could infect nail beds.

- Always wear a hat, preferably broad-brimmed.

- Apply sun cream before going outside.

- Wear earmuffs if using noisy equipment.

- Always wear protective eyewear when pruning, spraying, or grinding metal.

- Take a drink with you, as you would if you went to the gym or went for a bike ride.

- Buy knee pads and/or a kneeling pad to help those knees.

- Wear proper footwear, not open thongs or sandals, and never garden barefoot.

- Keep a basic first aid kit close by, especially for cuts and stings.

- Make sure one householder has learnt CPR, especially if there is a swimming pool. Be smart and leave a "pool noodle" in the pool.

- Avoid using ladders and if pruning, tie the ladder to a branch.

- Avoid accidents by not leaving tools or hoses lying around. Rakes have always had a terrible reputation.

- Always watch the weather reports, as gardening in an electrical storm is dangerous.

- Avoid planting bee-loving plants, for example, lavender (Lavandula angustifolia), near a pool.

- Running around a pool is forbidden.

- Ban all glassware around a pool.

- Always have an adult near a pool when children are swimming.

- Be aware of slippery steps and paths.

- Don't leave electrical appliances or extension leads around the garden, especially near a pool.

- If you have possums in your garden, be aware of the association between the Bairnsdale ulcer (the flesh-eating ulcer) and possum dung. Therefore, use gloves when picking up leaves and raked material, and don't kneel if your knees are bare.

- Garden earlier in the day when it is cooler and easier to work.

- BBQs are popular but should be placed away from eddying winds and should not be used on fire restriction days.

- Be careful handling fuel for your mower and hedging equipment, and only fill up in a safe area. Never fill up any tank if the motor is still hot. Just be patient and wait ten minutes.

- Filling up the tank of a lawnmower on the grass leaves a brown patch if you accidentally overfill the tank.

- Wear a bright coloured top when gardening outside your boundary (for example, when mowing your nature strip), to alert passing traffic. If you have an orange safety "dunce cap" (traffic cone), then leave it standing in the gutter as you work close by.

- Always make sure gates and fences are safe-proof.

- Fireproof your home (especially in rural Australia), with guidelines from local authorities. Remember, leaving "early" is always an option.

- Avoid planting thorny trees or shrubs anywhere in the garden (roses are excused).

- And finally, always wash your hands after gardening.

Final Thought

"Work smart, work safe, and lettuce have peas of mind."

"Always wash your hands after gardening"

HOW TO SELECT PLANTS

Plant selection is influenced by many factors. For example, the style of the house, advice from friends and others, and one's budget. Information from books, TV shows, and visits to nurseries and botanic gardens may also influence your choice. To make plant selection easier, we introduced the 5F rule, which represented the five things we wanted from a plant.

- Foliage
- Flowers
- Fragrance
- Fruit
- Freedom of disease

No plant could offer the 5Fs easily, but citrus plants came close, especially limes (Citrus x latifolia). The other advantage of the citrus group was its ability to hold its fruit longer than other fruit trees.

My tips and tricks

- Only buy those plants that offer three out of the 5Fs.
- Remember that reliability, maintenance requirements, invasiveness, and water needs are also important issues to consider when choosing plants.

"Only select plants that have at least three of the 5 F's"

FOLIAGE

FLOWERS

FRAGRANCE

FRUIT

FREEDOM OF DISEASE

Anecdote

A lady told me her husband said he would leave home if she bought any more plants. So, when I asked her the outcome, she told me how much she missed him.

Final Thought

"You can't buy happiness, but you can buy plants and that's pretty much the same thing."

SOIL

When a city like Melbourne is nearly two hundred years old, it is almost impossible to buy quality topsoil. Either it has been built on, or it was sold off years ago. Soil that is purchased today may look good, but it may have been sterilised. This happens during its heated preparation process, to remove any unwanted pathogens and weed seeds. It is now inert.

Have you ever pushed aside a small pile of leaves with your foot and noticed all of those useful little insects frolicking around? As they live and die, they add minerals and nutrients to your soil. Bought soil does not have any of these useful little "mates".

When landscaping, I rarely bought any soil because I knew that as I dug holes for the plants, I would have that additional soil to use elsewhere if needed.

Often, I see landscaping sites with mounds of "new" soil waiting to be barrowed in. The soil is then placed at the final bed height, and yes, what does one do with the excess soil once planting starts? I always had my pre-planting levels set at least ten centimetres below the proposed finishing height. The diggings would then fill up the beds and added mulch would then complete the desired height. The beds would always finish 2.5 centimetres below any paved area to prevent any washout. This way, there was no cost wastage in buying extra soil, carting it to the beds, removing the excess, and then paying for its removal.

You won't believe it, but the best soil you can ever have is already there, unless it contains problematic weeds like oxalis or onion weed. To enhance your home soil, just add fertiliser and abundant mulch. There are many different types of soil available if needed, but I would recommend buying loamy soil with equal parts of sand, silt, and clay, to which you can also add fertiliser and organic matter.

"Life's a garden, so dig it, as gardeners know all the dirt and a little dirt never hurt."

My tips and tricks

- Only buy new soil if you need it.

- The soil that accumulates whilst digging any hole can be spread around, in preference to making the garden beds look lumpy.

- Add as much organic matter as possible to your soil in the garden.

- Remember the soil in your garden is much better than you think.

- Add fresh animal manure (my preference is cow manure) to your soil if it is available. Allow six weeks before you start planting to avoid any root burn of new plants.

- Add trace elements (which come in a small plastic bag at your local nursery) to older gardens. These relatively cheap products contain calcium, iron, magnesium, and molybdenum, for example, for the depleted older gardens.

- Some plants are not grown in the commercially made potting mix but a heavier soil, often mountain soil. If their root balls dry out, they will become hard and then it will become difficult to rehydrate them. To prevent this issue, soak the root ball in a wheelbarrow full of water overnight. The next morning, gently "shake" the root ball and watch a lot of mountain soil wash away. Now plant with a little peat moss into the local soil and be ready for the emergence of the plant's vitality after avoiding a "rock hard" future.

- Checking the pH of your soil can be very important to clarify if your soil is in the ideal pH range of 5.5 to 7.5. There are plenty of probe-type kits, which are fairly accurate to give you a reading. Even though moisture and nutrients are important for plant growth, pH abnormalities will stop plants from absorbing the right minerals and trace elements for vigorous growth. A very, very simple guide to your soil's pH is to look at the vitality of existing plants in your garden and/or those growing in a neighbour's garden. If plant growth is poor, then check the pH. You can add sulphate of iron to lower the pH or lime and its slow-release form (dolomite lime) to raise the pH.

- "Soil" can be bought as potting mix, which is popular in container planting and propagation. Gardeners prone to respiratory disease should wear a mask and avoid sweeping up the ground where potting mixes have been used.

- Remember, loam was not built in a day.

Final Thought

*"Remember, anyone can have dirt,
but gardeners have soil."*

PLANTING TIPS

It is assumed that one has to just dig a hole and carefully place the plant in it, backfill, fertilise, and water it in. Sounds adequate, but read on, as correct planting techniques are essential.

It is no wonder that conscientious gardeners spend all day in their "beds" as they dig gardening.

My tips and tricks

- Choose the style of planting. For example, formal, informal, combined, or other.

- Check the spacing of plants to avoid overplanting, with the subsequent higher cost of purchase and plant competition for nutrients and moisture. Many people plant too closely, as if the plants may become lonely. I call this habit "emotional planting".

- Water your new plants when you get them home, as you may not have a chance to plant them until days later.

- Plant with others to have more fun, but remember that some gardening is not always done together.

> *"Plant and your spouse plants with you,*
> *weed and you weed alone."*

> —Jean-Jacques Rousseau

- Always fill up the hole first with water before you plant. Let it drain away and then plant. By following this advice, you will rarely lose a plant, as it has been planted in moist soil. If there is poor drainage, it will soon become apparent, as the water in the hole fails to be absorbed readily. This problem will need to be remedied before proceeding.

- Add some fertiliser into the hole before planting, mix it up, and then add the rest afterwards, sprinkling it around the drip line of the plant.

- Reduce the amount of fertiliser when growing vegetables in rotation, as they need less in this situation. For example, growing a crop of peas first will add nitrogen to the soil, which will then be available for the next crop of vegetables. Rotation planting lists are readily available.

- Companion planting can reduce certain bugs. For example, nasturtiums, when planted amongst vegetables, will reduce aphids, especially woolly aphids attacking an apple tree. Marigolds, when planted with tomatoes, reduce whitefly.

- Companion planting can also reduce water needs as more ground is covered with plants, thus reducing evaporation.

- Plant by the moonlight to find out if this is just an urban myth.

- Plant in groups of three or five for a more natural look.

- Plant vegetables in squares in preference to lines, as you can plant more in a square area.

- Stagger the amount of vegetables planted at any one time, so that the right amount is available when ready to be picked (that is, you can do regular harvesting). You can always "half harvest" some vegetables. This happens when you leave half a cucumber on the plant, the end covered in plastic wrap, picking the remaining half when you are ready.

- Only plant the vegetables you like and enjoy their freshness.

- Organic vegetables and fruit are achievable at home. As Michael Pollan said, *"If it came from a plant, eat it; if it is made in a plant, don't."*

- Older gardeners used to bury the liver of a calf or a sheep at the base of a passion fruit vine (Passiflora

'Nellie Kelly') before planting, with resultant vigorous growth. Chelated iron products now replace this method. Added compost is then the icing on the cake. Pavlova with passion fruit and cream, here I come! Yeah!

- Transplant any plant you need or want to, preferably after rainfall, and in the coolest months.

- Don't firm a new plant in with your bare fingers, where a cat may have buried its excrement. As mentioned before, fungal spores and sharp objects may also be lurking about.

Anecdote

Be sure that everyone knows which plant is to be transplanted. On one of my landscaping jobs, I had to leave the site for two hours. To make sure nothing could go wrong, I placed a red ribbon on all plants to be saved. When I returned, all the plants with red ribbons were removed and lying on the ground. My young "stallions" believed you could just replant them when they saw me react. I asked them all to leave the site immediately and run home as fast as they could, for their own safety. We made up the next day.

- Plant vegetables and herbs in the general garden as well, which then becomes the true "picking garden".
- Plant vegetables and herbs in any available "container" if space is a problem. For example, disused

potting mix bags, unused rubbish bins that have drainage holes, and in troughs or pots that may only find ideal space near the back door or on top of a carport. Yes, why not, as the carport roof is in full sun.

- Don't firmly pull on a plant that seems stuck in its plastic pot. Lay the pot gently on the ground, on its side, and press one's foot on it. Then slowly but easily remove the plant. Yes, this does work. Rarely do you need to cut the pot apart to remove its contents. For terracotta pots, run a knife around the root ball in an attempt to release it, in preference to breaking the pot to remove the plant.

- Gently tease but do not tear the roots off the root ball if the plant is pot bound.

- Do all of your plantings on a cooler day and earlier in the day, before it gets too hot.

- Plant hedges close to the road to "filter" fumes and reduce noise.

- Save time when you have a lot to plant. Place the plants correctly and dig all the holes without putting your spade down. Then plant up and backfill lastly. In this way, you don't put your spade down as you would when you plant one at a time. Over a day of planting, you would be surprised at the amount of time saved.

- As you plant, throw the empty pots onto the lawn, to make it easier to pick them up later. Any soil stuck in the pot bounces out as the pot hits the ground, often with some residual fertiliser. At the end of the day, the lawn is leaf raked and soon becomes a lot greener with the "crumbs" from the pots.

- Soak seeds overnight to help them germinate when planted. These can be placed on sheets of moist toilet paper, which is folded over and placed in a small furrow the next day and covered with soil.

"I wasn't all that interested in gardening, but I planted a few seeds, and it grew on me."

- Some people are prepared to nip larger seeds with nail clippers, to promote germination.

"Don't judge your day by the harvest you reap, but by the seeds you sow."

—Robert Louis Stevenson

- Just don't plant yourself in front of the TV.

Final Thought

"Good plants fit any hole."

FEEDING YOUR GARDEN

Feeding your garden should be a simple task. Enthusiastic gardeners, like chefs, have their own secrets, whilst nurseries have shelves full of recommended products. To keep it simple, just read on.

My tips and tricks

- Keep it very simple and feed your garden at least twice a year, on the first day of autumn and the first day of spring. These times are six months apart, which is easy to remember, and therefore perfect. Alternate an organic fertiliser with a granular product that is man-made.

- Understand that vegetable gardens require more frequent feeding, and if you have time, make it a liquid feed. This can come from diluted cow manure that has been stored in a large bin (with a lid on) for at least six weeks, or powdered products (which are mixed with water) from your nursery.

- Note that liquid feeding your garden is more suited in the winter months, where it is absorbed more readily than granular fertilisers. Use home-made vegetable broths as well.

- Add blood and bone (a powdered fertiliser) under mulches, especially woodchip mulch, to compensate for any nitrogen drain. Hoof and Horn is the choice powdered fertiliser, so buy it and use it when available.

- Dolomite lime is a great annual additive for your vegetable garden, as it is rich in calcium and magnesium.

- Foliage feeding is also a great way to feed plants, as their leaves can absorb essential minerals.

- Remember osmicated granules do not work well under 20° Celsius, so don't rely on them in winter.

- Feed all plants by scattering the chosen fertiliser under the plant's "drip line" and not near its centre or trunk.

- Take care of indoor plants. They need less fertiliser and water as they are living in reduced light. Don't waste any water and fertiliser down the laundry trough when you water your plants inside. Take them outside, and water and feed them as they sit in the garden. This way, any runoff ends up in the garden. Sometimes, a light hose spray of water can freshen up the foliage of an indoor plant that is taken outside.

<u>*Anecdote*</u>

I can remember my father's garden shed filled with at least twenty containers with different NPK (nitrogen, phosphorus, and potassium) ratios. Each container had the "secret formula" written on it. Instead of buying a five- or ten-kilogram bag of one ingredient, he would buy a twenty-five- or fifty-kilogram bag from an agricultural store. He was like a garden "master chef", giving perfectly grown roses, fruits, and vegetables to all who visited.

Final Thought

"*Early to bed, and early to rise, work hard in your garden, and don't forget to fertilise.*"

—Emily Whaley

WATERING YOUR GARDEN

I have found that more plants falter or die when they are overwatered, as opposed to being underwatered. Soil that is too wet is less oxygenated and plants are then deprived of it. Overwatering happens more frequently when homeowners have a sprinkler system, and they just want to "spoil" their plants. This overwatering creates large and annoying water bills, leaches fertiliser away, attracts more snails, increases more fungal diseases, and ultimately more plant stress, so why do it?

It was very interesting to see how plants coped with underwatering in recent severe droughts in Melbourne. Most plants coped, to the surprise of their owners and local nurseries, even when Stage 4A water restrictions were introduced.

Watering correctly depends on how much and how often. The amount of water needed relates to the surface area of a plant's foliage, which of course we are not going to measure. Obviously, a large tree will need a lot more water than a small shrub. Lawns (which consist of many small grass plants living close together) will also have different water needs, as will vegetable gardens.

If you can imagine, the soil consists of many particles with little spaces (pores) that are filled with oxygen, moisture, and nutrients. When you overwater, oxygen leaves these spaces and water fills them. As the water gets used or drains away, oxygen re-enters the spaces, unless you keep overwatering.

When the soil particles are only just covered with moisture and the pores are full of oxygen and nutrients, you have the ideal situation to create a plant's needs. This situation is called "vital capacity".

I have spent considerable time on this subject, more than is probably needed, because I wanted everyone to have healthier plants and lower water bills.

So, follow the advice below to see if I am right.

"Don't overwater me, just keep me moist"

My tips and tricks

- Water deeply and infrequently. Except for vegetable gardens, this means watering every fourteen days, for at least one hour per section of the garden. Let's face it, no one with an irrigation system will do this, so let's compromise and make it weekly. Just don't water every day!

- Try to water the ground and preferably not any flowers, which can easily be damaged. Plants without flowers are quite happy to have a little "shower" as well, so let them enjoy their moment, but only early in the day, to prevent residual droplets of water scorching leaves on a very hot day.

- Dish up the soil around plants (especially the newly planted ones), to create a "saucer" that can hold more water, and so reduce the runoff.

- Never water at night, as this attracts more snails, slugs, and fungal diseases. The reason we have watered so late is because we believed that the water pressure was better overnight. Our mothers also watered in the evening, because that was the only time they had, leading us to believe that watering late was the way to go. Technology can also give "incorrect" watering times, as many watering computers (from overseas) are pre-set for 2 a.m., making people believe that this is the best time to water.

- Adhere to the best watering times. My recommendations are 8 a.m. in winter and 5 a.m. in summer. Another great advantage of sticking to these times is that when you go outside in the morning, you may notice an area that is not wet, or a puddle lying close by, alerting you to a potential problem. Watering at night does not give you this information.

- You may not need to use your sprinkler system at all in the winter months. My sprinkler system in Melbourne is always turned off in June and rescheduled in late September, depending on natural rainfall, of course.

- Plants love a quick rinse, especially when rainfall is infrequent.

- Realise that old hoses can be drilled and turned into soaker hoses. Why not?

- Add small lengths of PVC or aggie drainage pipe into the root balls of plants in larger pots and also into very densely planted garden beds. Leave the top of the pipe just above ground level to assist with watering. Then fill the pipe directly with water, and yes, it is that easy.

- In Australia, it is not uncommon to have droughts, where the soil can dry out and become hydrophobic (repel water). There are many commercial products available that claim to facilitate water absorption and retention. Unfortunately, they have sometimes been associated with negative results. My recommendation is to add as much compost to the soil as possible and aerate the ground, to allow water penetration. Often old pieces of carpet can be left in place (like a doona cover) for a few days to help maintain moisture.

- Place old garden hoops strategically on the corners of garden beds to stop hoses from being dragged over beds and damaging any plants. Paint them yellow to remind you where they are.

- If your tap handle is stiff and hard to turn, add a small piece of split garden hose to the handle to make it larger, and experience the difference.

- Gardens that are heavily mulched hold moisture, and therefore need less watering.

- Plants in frost-prone areas should never be watered at night as they can ice up.

- Place a bucket under a hanging basket as you water it, to collect water and nutrients to be poured onto the garden.

- Remember, you need watering too, so regularly stop what you are doing and have a drink of water.

Don't forget the good old-fashioned water fights, but of course not with neighbours.

47

Final Thought

"I always wet my plants."

STAKING

This procedure should be straightforward, but often it is not. Rows of beautiful standard roses can be seen with stakes at different heights and in different positions. This idea that a stake can go in anywhere, or can be thick or thin, tall or short, will only diminish the aesthetics of your garden.

My tips and tricks

- Use stakes that are tubular, as these can be filled with water, whenever.

- When staking a plant that just needs one stake, try to place it at the back of the plant. The stakes are usually made of timber, metal, or bamboo and can be of various thicknesses, so choose the appropriate one.

- Stake before you plant a tree to prevent root damage, especially a bare rooted one.

- When two larger stakes are needed, usually for trees, they may need stronger ties, possibly made from hessian strips.

- Hit the stake in on a slight angle away from the plant, so when the two are drawn together, the stake will be vertical.

- Use a figure of eight knot when tying off, to prevent the stake from rubbing the trunk or damaging any part of the plant.

- You can make life easier by keeping a roll of string in a large, upturned pot sitting in the garden so that it is always readily available for tying off a plant.

- When staking standard roses, leave the stake ten centimetres higher than the trunk to prevent the rose head from snapping off in strong winds.

- Ties can be bought at hardware stores or can easily be made out of disused pantyhose, cut into strips. Any old bike wheel tubes can be cut into long strips and become very useful ties, especially for trees.

- Any sturdy fallen branches make perfect rustic stakes in a vegetable garden. A tripod of old branches can look great supporting a tomato plant, beans, or sweet peas (Lathyrus odoratum).

- You can paint the stakes any colour you like to add an artistic outcome, green being the most popular. Others believe that painted stakes last longer.

- Keen gardeners wash and sterilise the tips of stakes after use, prior to storing them in the shed.

- If a stake is hard to remove, hammer it in a little further and you will find it is much easier to pull out.

- Remove all stakes when they are no longer needed.

<u>*Anecdote*</u>

I once suggested using pantyhose to a client and came back to see she had used the whole pantyhose on one plant. Not a good look.

Final Thought

"There is nothing like a good steak and a home-grown salad."

COMPOST/MULCH

Compost is the supreme garden food and soil improver. It has also proven it is okay to "bury" the past.

Keen gardeners have always kept any kitchen scraps (excluding any meat or bones), lawn clippings, some weeds, leaves, straw, and any other vegetative matter including torn-up newspapers for the compost bin. Remember, fallen leaves are like nature's little butterflies and a gift, so rake them up. By layering different components and adding animal manure when available, the result is a very desirous mulch.

This can then be distributed around the garden to a depth of approximately seven centimetres. Real enthusiasts, and there are plenty of them, have different bins at different stages of decomposition, for future use. They enthusiastically turn the contents of the bin over and over or aerate the heap by plunging old broom handles into it, to accelerate the decomposing process. Most gardeners allow six months before their compost is ready to use as mulch.

Bins vary, but I prefer the open system (the aerobic approach), where a sheet of welded mesh forms an open cylinder, approximately 1.2 metres high. Others prefer a plastic bin with a lid (the anaerobic approach), as they believe there are fewer flies, and rodents can't gain entry. All compost bins perform best if they don't dry out and are not placed in a shady spot, which slows the process.

Other types of composting do not use bins at all but include methods like trenching. This is where organic material is placed in a trench in the ground, and when the trench is almost full, it is totally covered with soil. The same method can be done by digging holes anywhere when space for a compost area is limited. Others put their excess material (usually leaves) into plastic bags and leave the bags aside in the sun for three months, before spreading it onto the garden as leaf mould.

Traditionally, compost areas were placed down the back of the garden, out of the way, but the rules are changing.

My tips and tricks

- If you use the welded mesh method, keep the hinged part to the front, for easy access.

"Compost is proof that there is life after death"

- Grow some nasturtiums on a piece of lattice to hide your bin if you don't like the look.

- Be creative and put a smaller compost bin or bins in the front garden, behind a large shrub, so that it is out of sight. Not taking organic material to the back garden and later having to bring the mulch back saves a lot of time. This tip really does work, so try it.

- There is no reason why excess leaves can't be raked directly onto garden beds as a "winter blanket". This happens readily in nature and saves a lot of time carting large piles of leaves to the compost bin.

- When distributing the mulch around your garden, avoid placing it too close to a tree's trunk or the centre of a shrub. Leave a small area, approximately 150 millimetres wide, mulch free. Some keen gardeners place a "ring" of sand, to keep any mulch from affecting the bark of a tree or shrub. This way, you are only mulching the ground.

- Remember to collect excess leaves trapped in guttering. If large trees create massive autumn drops, then add these to the compost bin.

- Wet large piles of leaves first, as they are easier to pick up, and at the same time, you can get more into your wheelbarrow. An added advantage is that wet leaves decompose more quickly.

- Kill any compost odour with shredded newspaper, layered throughout.

- "Compost starters" are available to buy commercially to activate your compost heap. They often contain essential microbes. Otherwise, just alternate your layers in the compost bin with green matter (lawn clippings), followed by a layer of brown matter (old leaves) and then some animal manure, if available. If you have kept some of the previous decomposed heap, then throw some of it onto the new heap as the fourth layer. Mother Nature now takes over.

- "Green" composting occurs when a green nitrogen-fixing plant (for example, peas) is grown first and then turned into the soil. Six weeks later, plant another vegetable and listen to the worms saying thank you.

- Keen gardeners sometimes grow vegetables in a bale of hay if they don't have a garden bed or directly into a full compost bin. They create a space and then add some enriched soil before planting their seedlings or pumpkin seeds. These young plants then gain their nourishment as they grow in their new "home".

- Mulching machines are available commercially and the shredded material readily decomposes more quickly. Apart from the noise and fuel handling, they can be very useful, especially in larger gardens.

- Male urine added to a compost bin works best. Don't ask me why.

- Those gardeners who don't compost can buy any of the bagged mulch products (for example, baled hay, pea straw, lucerne hay, or sugar cane), as they all perform well. These products are spread around to a depth of ten centimetres. My favourite is lucerne hay, as it adds nitrogen to the soil without growing seedlings, as pea straw does. I avoid woodchip products (including sawdust), as they drain the soil of nitrogen as they decompose.

- Bulk products are available from garden supply companies, such as mushroom compost, which looks great. Just keep it away from acid-loving plants such as azaleas, camellias, and rhododendrons.

- Other gardeners who don't make home-made mulch and don't buy bagged or baled products, may buy and lay decorative pebbles or small stones as mulch. If you do, lay them on a weed mat or shade cloth first, to avoid them getting mixed up with the soil. Although pebbles last longer than other mulches, they eventually get mixed in the soil, or get littered with leaves and eventually have weeds growing in them, making them high maintenance. My advice is to only use them on top of pots, to stop soil being blown away, or in Japanese gardens as a design feature.

Anecdote

There are many special compost/mulch products on the market. The best product I have ever seen was made in Tasmania, Australia. Here, the remnants of a fish called Orange roughy (a deep ocean, extremely ugly fish) are filleted and the rest is trashed (approximately 80 per cent). This was then mixed with woodchips and composted over a few months. The end product was then bagged and sold through large garden outlets. Guess what it was called? "Fish 'n' Chips"! How clever. So all of you with "fertile" minds, create something similar.

Final Thought

"Compost is proof that there is life
after death."

WEEDING

"Do you, Gardener, take this garden, to weed from this day forth?"

Weeds, as mentioned earlier, are unwanted plants whose virtues are yet to be explained. They never grow in straight lines and rob nutrients and moisture from gardens without asking. They are always in the wrong place and intend to stay there. If left alone, they will seed, and one year of seed will be seven years of weeds.

Either you put a sign on the front of the house saying, "Free weeds, pick your own", or follow my advice below.

My tips and tricks

- Become "fired up" to know that the best and cheapest weed killer in town is boiling water. Yes, boiling water! How simple is that?

"The hottest weed killer in town"

USE BOILING WATER

- Stay excited to know that apple cider vinegar is also a great weed killer when sprayed on weeds.

- Smother techniques (for example, using sheets of cardboard, newspaper, or a thick tarpaulin) work well. Leave in position for at least eight weeks. Some people leave the newspaper or cardboard in place, pierce holes in it, and then plant their vegetable seedlings. The paper and cardboard then act as a "blanket" of mulch, helping to retain moisture.

- Stay vigilant after you have weeded a bed. Use a hoe regularly, as this will turn over any germinating weeds. This is a very effective activity as you sing, "Yo hoe, yo hoe, it's off to work we go". This technique allows you to stay ahead of the weeds.

- Dig the bed over so that the weeds are now underground, almost the same as trench mulching. Believe me, this is a very quick weeding technique, as the buried weeds are now a source of nutrients for other plants.

- Never use plastic sheets to smother weeds, as it prevents oxygen, nutrients, and water from entering the soil, whilst discouraging all the soil's inhabitants, worms, and insects.

- Don't waste your money on weed mats, as the weeds eventually grow on top of them.

- When landscaping, we used to scalp off the top five centimetres of soil containing the weeds and seeds, and then discard it, or we left it in a pile next to the compost bin. As the weeds rot, this soil can be added to the compost bin in layers. This scalping method was the greatest time saver on site, in contrast to hand weeding.

- Avoid commercial weedicides if you can, thus becoming environmentally responsible.

- Not all weeds are undesirable. Some weeds have a "culinary opportunity", where their leaves and or flowers are added to salads. Daisies, chickweed, fat hen, and even onion weed are sometimes eaten by people I don't know. You have my permission to eat them.

- Add a thick layer of mulch where you can, to smother some small young germinating weeds.

- You can try a commercial "flame thrower" for weeds. This is connected to a gas cylinder and ignited to create a small flame to burn the weeds, but the roots don't always die. This is very effective, just be careful.

- With challenging noxious weeds, for example, onion weed (Allium triquetrum) or oxalis species (Oxalis pes-caprae or Oxalis articulata), persistent weeding or weedicides rarely offer good results. The cheapest way to resolve the problem is to excavate the affected soil, usually to a depth of twenty millimetres, and discard it. A small amount of "new soil" may need to be purchased or salvaged from other parts of the garden to fill the bed up. Some people spend hours over many days trying to remove the small corms, becoming frustrated and annoyed, not knowing there is a simpler answer to removing those noxious weeds: excavation.

- Don't laugh, because weeds can become very useful, as they are high in nitrogen. You probably won't try this method, but you can boil the weeds for an hour in a large pot. When cool, strain the liquid and pour it on your garden as a liquid fertiliser. Stop laughing now.

Final Thought

*"To weed or not to weed, that
is the garden."*

UNDERSTANDING BUGS

There is only one thing worse than finding a worm in your apple, and that is finding half a worm. However, some famous horticulturalists prefer to share the apple with a caterpillar than use pesticides.

We can also change our attitude as we get older, and not rush for our pesticides every time, as there are other practical solutions that can protect our garden. So let us agree that we are all really "green", just different shades of green, and we can collectively influence our environmental destiny, and at the same time, show our children and grandchildren the way. We know this is worth doing, as we are constantly reminded that some popular pesticides and weedicides that were considered safe have now been closely associated with human disease, whilst their long-term impact on the environment is yet to be revealed.

This section of my book is the most challenging, as all garden centres and hardware stores have far too many chemical products ready for sale, not always understanding their core responsibility to the environment. Once purchased, these products are frequently used incorrectly and without consideration for health and safety issues. In many garden sheds at home, one can see all of the unused, expensive pesticides and weedicides lined up for future use, and guess where they finish up when out of date?

Fortunately, there are easier ways of managing bugs that are worth trying first.

To make it simpler, I have decided to add some information first, by looking at the three most common garden pests (bugs).

Insects

If "bugs" have wings and legs, they are insects. So yes, use a preferably organic insecticide. For example, a solution of crushed onion and garlic with some chilli powder.

Fungi

If plants have powdery-looking leaves, spots on their leaves, or leaves that are rolled up, then fungi are involved. So yes, use a fungicide, preferably an organic one. For example, one tablespoon of baking soda to four litres of water, and then spray it on.

Chewers

If the leaves are eaten from the edge, it is probably from caterpillars. If the leaf is eaten from the edge and has holes in it, then it is usually from snails and slugs. Now bring out the beer to drown them, as they can't resist the yeast.

If a leaf has been chomped, it is usually by possums in the city or kangaroos in the country. Usually, these animals leave a "poop" trail that confirms their whereabouts.

Simplifying the list of the most common bugs, as I have done above, is to help people identify the most common problems more easily, thus decreasing chemical purchases and encouraging simpler choices every time.

My tips and tricks

- Try to identify the "bug" before you do anything.

- Learn how to make the most effective organic insecticides and fungicides.

- If the impact of a bug is minimal, it may be smarter to just live with the problem in preference to buying expensive products that are overused in the garden.

- Have a party and give snails and slugs some beer as a special treat. You can finish the rest.

- Always find simple non-chemical answers first. For example, shooting a strong jet of water from a hose at aphids to break a few legs or wings, or squashing a few caterpillars, may be all that is needed.

- Discard any branches from diseased plants intelligently, by placing them in a sealed plastic bag and sending them off to landfill.

- Prevention is also important. For example, don't water at night. This will reduce fungal problems, especially black spots and powdery mildew on roses.

- Keep plants healthy as plants are like humans; they have more resilience when healthy. So, feeding and watering techniques are crucial in maintaining a healthy garden.

- Consider alternating any treatments you have chosen to avoid resistance, especially when using antifungal sprays.

- Understand that other different bugs can cause problems for plants. Although rare, viruses and bacteria can attack plants. The best control here is to avoid taking any cuttings from these diseased plants and also to keep the plants as healthy as possible as a preventative measure, as mentioned above.

- Give your little four-legged friends a treat. Possums are best handled by providing an alternative and appealing food choice. Spreading blood and bone or Vicks VapoRub (a camphor-based ointment for coughs and colds) over their pathways may deter them. Some people have success with ornamental owls or aluminium pie trays hanging in the trees. Others use a product called Poss-Off, and others swear that spraying ammonia over any possum pathways works wonders. Good luck!

• Keen gardeners prefer to scratch the trunk of an infected tree, and then paint the "wound" with a systemic insecticide (which is absorbed into the plant's tissues) in preference to spraying the whole plant, with its over-spraying issues. Others drill holes in the lower trunk of a very large tree where regular spraying is impractical and inject an insecticide.

Final Thought

"Don't let little things bug you."

SPRAYING

Gardeners have used spray cans for a long time to control garden pests and have also made up chemical solutions for their spraying equipment. My advice is simple: spray less. But if you do spray, read on.

My tips and tricks

- Always wear a mask and gloves when spraying.

- Always read the label first.

- Only use the recommended dose, not more.

- Only spray on days when there is no wind.

- When spraying, remember to spray the underside of the foliage as well, as this is where the problem often lies.

- Protect adjacent plants from overspray by using a flat piece of cardboard as a shield. Plants can also be protected using large rubbish liner bags or using an upturned rubbish bin.

- Clean equipment after use and store it safely, especially any chemicals.

- Discard empty bottles properly, and don't reuse them.

- Keep a log of your spraying activities.

- Check the withholding time of any chemicals used before picking any fruit or vegetables.

- Wash hands and face thoroughly after finishing and discard your mask.

- Home-made organic products are the best, so always try them first.

Final Thought

"A Who's Who of pesticides is a concern for us all."

"GO ANTS GO"

Where there is one ant, there are probably a thousand more. With over twelve thousand species of ants worldwide, it is no wonder that most people don't like them, especially if they are found in the kitchen.

Although there are companies dedicated to ant removal, it is hard to find a company that has the least toxic products. So, try any of the following tips first.

My tips and tricks

- Avoid leaving any food or food scraps on the kitchen benches.

- Avoid leaving unwashed dinner plates around. It is best to rinse them and place them in the dishwasher.

- Try to locate any cracks or crevices that allow entry and seal them off, usually with silicone gel.

- Use a 50/50 mix of vinegar and water as a spray or wipe.

- Lemon juice, cinnamon, or cayenne pepper are good alternatives.

- Boiling hot water may seem brutal, but it is very effective, especially outside.

- Plant mint bushes (peppermint appears to be the favourite), around the house as a deterrent.

- Check that pot plants are kept moist, as an ant nest is often found in pots with dry root balls. Often, scale insects attacking a stressed plant are the first warning of ant infestation.

- Leave a lemon rind on top of pots that have an ant infestation, as a deterrent.

Final Thought

"If ants are such busy workers, how come they find time to go to all the picnics?"

—Marie Dressler

LAWNS AND LAWN CARE

A green lawn has always had great appeal, yet its final appearance has always challenged us.

Lawns provide spaces for family recreation and relaxation, whilst their greenness complements any colourful garden beds. Many people are happy to mow anything green regardless of the quality of the lawn, whereas others would love a lawn like a bowling green.

As soil conditions and weather vary all over Australia, so do the lawn varieties suitable for your climate and the care they need. Hence, you will only need to have some basic tips and tricks to have a lawn that you are proud of.

My tips and tricks

- Select the right grass for your climate.

- Select a tougher grass like Kikuyu if heavy traffic from children at play eventuates.

- If shade is an issue, buffalo lawns will make a better choice.

- Only cut the lawn when it is dry.

- Don't cut the lawn too short as it will weaken it, with weeds invading shortly after. Leave it longer in summer, especially around trees.

- Keep lawn clippings (as they are high in nutrients) and add them to the compost bin. And remember to layer it with other vegetation, like leaves.

- Keep the lawn as healthy as possible. As lawns have a long growing season in warmer climates, they will benefit from more feeding and coring, and occasionally dethatching. Sometimes you can buy "aerating shoes" (with metal spikes attached to the sole), at larger garden stores that aerate the lawn as you walk all over it. This procedure works best after rain. Otherwise, hire a commercial aerator and share this cost with neighbours who may also plan to aerate their lawns.

- Water lawns deeply and infrequently, not every day.

- Feed lawns at least twice a year, with early spring and a lighter feed in late February being ideal in Australia. If you use granular fertiliser, water it in by hand to prevent burning.

- If you are repairing a bare patch of lawn, leave the lawn seed in the freezer overnight for two nights, and then sow. You will be surprised by seeing the seed germinating more quickly. Cover the patch being repaired with a small piece of shade cloth for three days, to minimise bird damage.

- Use a long plank of wood to help cut the lawn edges on straight runs or a garden hose for curved edges.

- Mowing strips, especially bricks laid on their side in mortar, can greatly reduce edge trimming time.

- If whipper snippers are to be used, then consider tree guards, especially home-made ones.

- Remove weeds from lawn manually, especially flat weeds, in preference to using weedicides.

- For those who don't want to go to the above effort, you can buy and lay synthetic turf, which can look amazing (for example, in a small courtyard). Avoid laying it close to large trees with vigorous roots that will soon become troublesome as they grow and distort the synthetic turf.

Anecdote

"My neighbour asked if he could use my lawnmower and I told him of course he could, so long as he didn't take it out of my garden."

—*Eric Morecambe*

Final Thought

"The grass is always greener when you water it."

PRUNING

A famous gardener, when asked when he pruned, answered "when I get the chance". I believe he meant a light prune is better than no prune at all. Pruning is an art in itself, but certain plants, like roses, are more forgiving than others when pruned by amateurs.

My tips and tricks for shrubs and trees

- Many winter and early spring flowering shrubs and trees like to be pruned after flowering, while most fruit trees (except stone-fruits) are traditionally pruned after autumn.

- Enthusiastic home gardeners like to thin out their fruit trees in early summer. This allows more light into the centre of the tree, growing slightly less but larger fruit, more than enough for a family.

- Embrace this piece of advice. When planting a new fruit tree, cut off any damaged roots. If any of the branches vary in length and thickness, then prune the thickest branches shorter than the others. These pruned pieces, when cut to the same length, can be "twirled" together and create "spacers" to open up the tree's framework.

- Avoid using ladders when pruning trees or tall shrubs, and if you must, always tie the ladder to a limb for safety. Always make sure the ground is as flat and stable as possible.

- Always make angled cuts.

- Reduce thicker branches in a two-way process to prevent tearing of the bark. Undercut the branch first and then reduce the limb. Then remove the stumpy bit last.

- "Wound" paint is recommended on larger wounds.

- Don't be reluctant to prune or clip evergreen shrubs and trees, as they are more vigorous with regular shaping.

Anecdote

An apprentice of mine was very strong and impatient. He went to cut down a large, unwanted shrub in one piece. As the shrub fell to the ground, he lost his balance and fell into the pool. He totally disappeared, but I willingly rescued him when he resurfaced.

Final Thought

"Get out on a limb; that's where all the fruit is."

My tips and tricks for roses

Some rose pruners just "nibble" their roses when pruning, whereas others cut back at least a third of the height. My technique is as follows:

- Sterilise your secateurs both before you start and after you finish your pruning.
- Remove any dead wood.
- Remove any spindly growth or criss-crossing branches.
- Reduce the height at least a third, cutting the thickest branches lower.
- Always angle cut each branch to an outside bud.
- Use any of the cuttings as spacers if needed, to open up the rose bush. Spacers are small pieces of a pruned branch that look like the letter Y when trimmed to the desired length. The bottom end is pierced by a

thorn on one branch, and the Y-shaped end is placed under a thorn of an adjacent branch, gently pushing the branches apart. Leave the spacer in place for at least six months.

- Enthusiasts use wound paint. Any non-leaded paint can be used.

- Discard rose cuttings immediately and never put them in the compost bin.

- Spray all roses and the surrounding soil after pruning with winter or pest oil and a natural antifungal.

- With summer pruning (to get the best autumn blooms or when planning for a special date to have blooms at their best), stress the rose by ceasing watering for three weeks. Then prune back lightly, taking a third of the plant. Then feed and water again. Approximately fifty days later, you will have the blooms back, at their best, ready for that special event—a wedding, a birthday, or a rose show.

- When pruning climbing roses, keep the thick stems attached to a wall or pergola. Trim back flowering twigs in summer. In winter, cut back leaders and laterals by about a third. Preserve any new long shoots to ultimately replace old growth.

- When pruning miniatures or ground cover roses, just use shears.

<u>*Anecdote*</u>

It is hard to believe that the most popular plant sold in our nursery was a rose. You would not think that a deciduous plant that has thorns, bugs (like aphids), and fungal diseases and needs so much attention would be so popular.

We used to have a sign at the nursery for Valentine's Day that said, "Don't give her roses, just give her the whole bush". It worked, as our roses were beautiful and at their best at that time.

Final Thought

"My garden rose to the occasion."

CONTAINER PLANTS

Container plants require special skills to maintain their vigour and have them looking their best all of the time. Whether you have a balcony garden, a courtyard garden, or some large plastic pots growing vegetables on your carport roof, the same issues appear. The most common issue that threatens a container plant is its root ball drying out and becoming too hard to rehydrate. In all my years of landscaping, I rarely found the root balls of larger pot plants adequately moist.

Clients always told me they had watered their containers every day, and they were sure that the root balls were moist. What they didn't realise is that the root balls start to shrink due to the sun on the pot, and in time, the root ball shrinks even further if not remedied. This creates a small space between the root ball and its container for water to escape too easily.

My tips and tricks

- Select square pots or troughs for stability in preference to conical ones, especially where there is wind. This tip is a really smart one.

- Attractability, suitability, stability, durability, desirability, availability, movability, and affordability give one the "ability" to choose the correct container every time.

- Drainage should be good but does not need to be perfect. We don't need water running away too quickly. We want to keep the root ball moist, at all times.

- Paint the inside of the concrete or terracotta container with waterproof paint to reduce the leaching of chemical products or fertilisers. It's worth the effort.

- Place large containers on small feet made from pieces of lattice or plastic or onto plant stands to help with drainage. This also helps keep the paving close by dry and not slimy, as there is now a little ventilation.

- Have heavier pots on wheels for easier shifting or use rollers when needed.

- Group containers together, especially herb pots, to reduce the sun's heat drying out an individual pot and its root ball.

"Have pot selection ability"

ATTRACTABILITY

SUITABILITY

STABILITY

DURABILITY

DESIRABILITY

AVAILABILITY

MOVABILITY

AFFORDABILITY

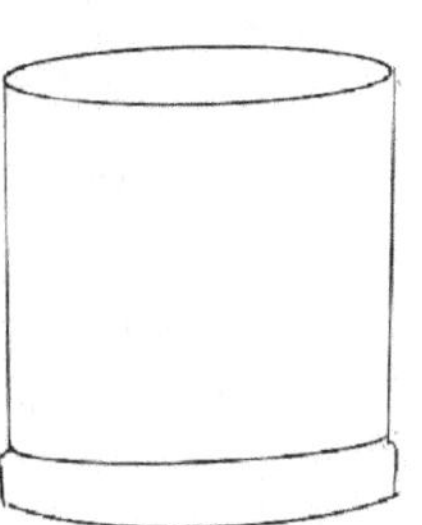

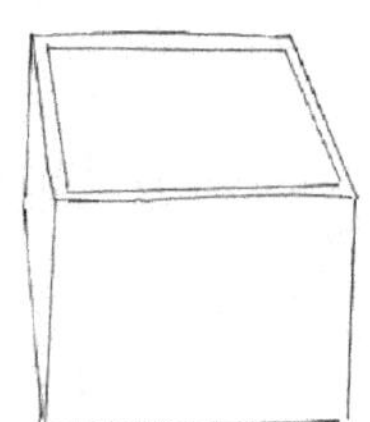

- Cover the drainage hole with used coffee filters or a piece of shade cloth. This stops bugs from entering the container and prevents soil from falling out and soiling the paving.

- Use enriched quality potting mix to give the chosen plant its best opportunity for good health.

- To lighten large pots and save on expensive potting mix, add broken pieces of polystyrene boxes as a filler (I recommend filling the bottom one-third). Used soft drink cans or plastic bottles can do the same job as a filler. If weight is still a problem, then select from a large range of plastic designer pots or GRC (glass-fibre reinforced concrete) containers.

- Select plants that are less vigorous in their growth habit, so they don't outgrow their pot too soon, or you will be repotting more frequently.

- Feed plants regularly with osmicated granules in the warmer months, when the granules work better, and liquid fertilisers at other times, to compensate for the leaching of nutrients.

- Use small pebbles or shells to cover the soil, so it won't blow away on windy balconies.

- To prevent root balls from drying out, leave a hose dripping on the container overnight every fortnight in the warmer months. Smaller pots can be dunked in a bin full of water until the root ball has stopped bubbling. Sometimes larger pots need to be tipped over carefully, and after their drainage holes have been plugged temporarily, stood up and filled with water until their root balls have also stopped bubbling.

You will be surprised by how effective this technique is. This can be done every couple of months in the warmer months. You may need the help of others. Don't forget to remove the plug.

- Self-watering containers are now available, and these may suit your needs.

- Water granules can be added to pots that are starch-based and form a gel that can hold 80 per cent more than their own weight.

- Cut up old sponges or non-soiled nappies and place them in any containers, including hanging baskets, to retain moisture as mentioned above. If you can be bothered, add used tea bags to also help hold moisture.

- You can always add small lengths of plastic drainage pipe with its tip showing so that you can fill these with water to try and keep larger root balls moist.

- Try to keep the size of the plant matching the size of its container so that it looks in balance. Plants that grow too quickly, are too tall, or are not pruned regularly will increase the chance of the container blowing over in the wind, with possible damage to plant and pot. A plant thrives better when its size is kept similar to the size of its container (that is, its nutrient base).

- Plant saucers are not really useful. Large saucers under heavy pots always seem to crack and are expensive to replace, so best not to invest in any.

Final Thought

*"A happy plant loves moist
(but not wet) feet."*

MOVING HEAVY ITEMS

Fortunately, there are many ways to move heavy pots, landscaping materials, and compost.

In the old days, a garden trolley (originally called a sack trolley) was used to move large sacks of coal or manure. In recent times, the same trolley can be used in many ways around the house and the garden.

My tips and tricks

- Firstly, you can place the heavy item on a trolley and push it forward with two hands, like pushing a pram.

- Secondly, if the item is too tall (for example, a tall pot of bamboo), then push the trolley along on a

45° angle, with one hand on one handle as you walk alongside, as if walking a dog.

- Thirdly, you can pull the trolley (when laden) behind you with both hands, like a horse and cart, especially on an upward slope.

- Fourthly, with assistance, you can place a very tall object on the trolley in a restricted space and just push the trolley forwards without tilting it back, whilst a helper is in front of the tall pot pulling the trolley forwards.

- Finally, you can lay the trolley flat and use it like a stretcher (with the help of others), especially when there is uneven ground or steps.

- Another useful trick for moving something heavy is to place the heavy object on a strong tarpaulin and pull it into position with or without the use of a ramp.

- Rollers made of wood (for example, old broomstick handles), or metal pipes can be used as rollers. These need to be approximately 1.2 metres long and should be placed on the ground. The heavy object is now lifted onto the rollers. As you move forward, reload the rollers.

"Here comes Mr. Jolly Trolley"

Final Thought

*"So have a jolly good time with
your trolley."*

INDOOR PLANTS

Indoor plants can provide great decorative opportunities, but few people have success in selecting the right ones or keeping them healthy. Often, they are bought on impulse, without knowing the plant's light, watering, and feeding requirements.

They are essentially "outdoor plants" brought inside, where their needs are now different.

My tips and tricks

- Understand that the fewer you have, the better. A few larger ones are better than lots of smaller ones.

- Always balance the size of the plant with the size of its container.

- Choose the right position (usually where there is good light but no direct sunlight).

- Some ventilation at times is acceptable, especially in air-conditioned homes.

- Keep plants moist but not wet. Owners are sometimes too conscientious and overwater their indoor plants. Sometimes, checking the weight of the plant by lifting it will indicate if it feels "light" and watering is needed. In contrast, many people water their indoor plants too often, usually on the same day each week, and this bad habit can also adversely affect the plants' vitality.

- Choose reliable plants, for example:
  - Madonna lilies (Spathiphyllum sp.)
  - Indoor ficus (Ficus "Fiddle Leaf" or Ficus benjamina)
  - Cymbidium orchids (Cymbidium sp.)
  - Moth orchids (Phalaenopsis spp.)
  - Cast iron plant (Aspidistra elatior), which is almost indestructible.
  - Some ferns and the Kaffir lily (Clivia miniata), when in full flower, can come inside happily.

- Liquid feeding every two months should be adequate.

- Check these plants for pests, as they are more prone to diseases living inside under stress. Look for scale insects as this is a common problem, and spray with pest oil if needed. Mealybugs are also common and persistent on indoor plants. Wash off most bugs at the sink. Touch others with alcohol on a cotton bud or spray them with Neem oil. If the indoor plant is riddled with mealybugs, it is smarter and cheaper to discard it and buy a new one.

- Indoor plants enjoy a little "holiday" outside, in a protected area, for at least two weeks. Often, a spray with water from your hose washes away any dust and freshens them up.

- Holiday plant care may require plants to be placed on very wet towels in a sink or bath. "Wick" watering can also keep a plant happy for three weeks.

- Spray foliage with very diluted white oil, to freshen up the foliage and give the leaves a sheen.

- Christmas trees hold their foliage longer if sugar is added to their watering source.

Final Thought

"Don't lose your 'impatience' with indoor plants."

FILLING A GAP WHEN
A PLANT OR PARTIAL PLANT DIES

Occasionally, a plant dies in the garden when in a row of similar plants, or half of it dies. Often, there is no apparent reason. There is now an obvious gap to spoil the garden's looks, a bit like a missing tooth.

My tips and tricks

- Bring long and flexible adjacent branches from existing plants as close together as possible to fill the gap, using a fishing line or its equivalent to tie the branches together. Leave the line in place and remove it after nine months. You will be surprised how soon the gap fills up.

- Plant a similar smaller plant and be patient.

- Plant a good filling creeper to fill the gap up quickly. For example, Star jasmine (Trachelospermum jasminoides) frequently blends in well.

- Place an ornament or its equivalent in the gap to create a focal point.

- Enlarge the gap to fit an old door on the fence to create a sense of artistic mystery.

Final Thought

"Plants don't need a gap year."

CORRECTING A SHRUB'S SHAPE

Sometimes a special plant has been squashed between other plants over the years and you want to save it.

My tips and tricks

- Place a stake close to the flattened side and pull any available branches toward the stake. Tie it off (pantyhose strips are ideal) and leave it for twelve months. Trim the other side of the plant if needed. You will be surprised by the ultimate result.

104

Final Thought

"Just stay in shape."

PROTECTING TREE TRUNKS

Tree trunks can easily be damaged whilst mowing, by hyperactive children, or the hot sun.

My tips and tricks

- Create a "no mow" zone, approximately one metre in diameter around trees in the lawn to prevent damage from the mower.

- Paint any serious trunk wounds with a special product sold at nurseries, or use the lead-free paint found in your shed.

- Place a commercial tree guard around the trunk or make one from an old plastic bottle.

- For young fruit trees, protect their trunks from being sunburned in the scorching sun by tying some cardboard or its equivalent around the trunk for the first year.

Final Thought

"Don't bark at me."

TREE ROOT PROBLEMS

Tree roots perform many vital functions, like supplying moisture and nutrients for the foliage above, whilst offering stability against strong winds. Without a functional and healthy root system, a tree will soon die. Other times, a tree's roots can have a majestic appearance at its base, for example, the Moreton Bay fig (Ficus macrophylla). These large roots spread out like an octopus under the tree's canopy and create a mystical appearance.

For most people, tree roots spell trouble, causing damage to the paving, driveways, footpaths, terracotta plumbing, and house or fence foundations.

You may have noticed a tree's roots in your nature strip rarely shows through, whilst the same tree's roots can wreck the adjacent footpath. This occurs once a tree's roots are covered with a non-porous material used for the footpath, like concrete or bitumen. The roots will do whatever is necessary to break through to get some oxygen, moisture, and nutrients.

My tips and tricks

- Only pave under small trees (up to six metres tall) that do not have very vigorous or large roots.

- Do your homework and select the right plants. There are larger trees that can cope better with root pruning than other smaller ones.

- Try to keep any paving three metres from the trunk. Fill the space with ground covers, bulbs, gravel, and furniture or a circular tree seat.

- Use a root control barrier (available at large hardware stores) when appropriate.

- Prune the canopy of a troublesome tree, if it is practical to do so. This reduces the volume of roots needed to support a larger tree and may now allow paving to take place more readily. This technique is similar to the bonsai approach.

- Understand tree roots. A tree's roots run out from the trunk a lot further than you think (approximately one and a half times the height of the tree). Also, approximately 90 per cent of a tree's roots are in the top one metre of soil, as tree roots prefer to travel horizontally in pursuit of nutrients and moisture. Because the volume of tree roots is so close to the surface, you can visualise the size of potential problems.

- Do taproots really exist? As a landscaper, I rarely saw any.

- You can also remove the number of tree roots carefully to allow smaller plants a better chance of survival by reducing competition for moisture and nutrients. Just don't overdo it.

- "Root pruning" is another technique that can take place weeks or months before a plant is to be removed and re-sited to a more favourable position in the garden. Just use a sharp spade or shovel and cut the root ball approximately forty centimetres from its trunk. If the root ball is any larger, because the plant is larger, the plant may be hard to shift without machinery. Water any plant to be shifted weeks before and feed with seafood fertiliser after it has been replanted. The best time to move a plant is after rain and in winter.

Anecdote

I once saw a hundred-year-old weeping elm tree (Ulmus glabra) moved to a more appropriate site after its main roots were boxed up for two years. Its root ball, when shifted by a crane, was four metres wide. Thirty years later, it is still a beautiful specimen.

Final Thought

"Never forget your roots."

MAMA'S HOME-MADE PLANT FOODS

There are no secrets with Mama, in the kitchen or outside.

Mama's tips and tricks

- Keep all the kitchen vegetable scraps and boil them up in a large pot for a couple of hours. When cool, pour this "liquid fertiliser" onto your pot plants or the garden. Normally, these scraps would go to the compost bin or landfill.

- Long pieces of citrus rind can be stored in a jar of icing sugar and water, instead of being thrown out. They can then be used to decorate cakes or added to cocktail drinks.

"Mama's homemade liquid fertiliser, from vegetable offcuts"

- Buy bagged cow manure, and then place a full bag in a large bin of water that has a lid. Months later, Mama's brew is ready. Now dilute one cupful of the brew per nine litres of water. Pour it onto your garden, especially your vegetable garden.

- Mama also says to keep some weeds, as they are rich in nitrogen. Crazy, but that's what Mama said. As mentioned earlier, weeds can also be boiled up and then poured over your vegetable garden as an enriched liquid fertiliser.

- Dig a sloping trench in a very large garden and place a quality tarpaulin in it. Place all grass clippings (which are high in nutrients) on top, and wet them with a hose (the "Boer Method"). With the aid of rain, there will soon be a runoff of enriched liquid. When collected, it can be diluted and used on your garden or lawn. This is a job for Mario, not Mama.

- Recycle eggshells as they are a great source of calcium. Place them in a blender first, then spread them over your vegetable garden.

- Make sure Mama does not get too "egg-cited".

Anecdote

If you want to meet Mama, then let me know, as she lives next door to Mother Nature.

Final Thought

"A smiling garden is a happy garden with Mama."

DEADHEADING AGAPANTHUS
(Agapanthus orientalis)

A sea of agapanthus in bloom, in a row along a driveway or planted under a tree en masse, is a spectacular summer event. Deadheading them can be laborious and back-breaking.

My tips and tricks

- Save time, and just pull the spent flower stalks with a bit of a jerk, and out pops the old, unwanted stalk. This technique works best with the miniature varieties and saves hours of work when you have many plants. Sometimes a few leaves may come out too, but this does not matter.

- If you use secateurs, then cut the stalks at their base.

- Enjoy the stalks as a cut flower. They last longer after dipping their cut ends in boiling water for fifteen seconds.

Final Thought

"To pull or not pull, that is the question."

PANTYHOSE
IN THE GARDEN

Not all pantyhose need to finish up in a landfill, as they are of great use in the garden.

My tips and tricks

- Cut the pantyhose up into strips to be used as garden ties.

- Store some vegetables (for example, onions), in the legs of pantyhose.

- Use pantyhose legs to sieve liquids used in the garden.

Final Thought

"Old gardeners never die; they just get tied up."

POT SWAPPING

This is a very clever technique where buried empty plastic pots are left in the ground, for example, under a large tree.

My tips and tricks

- "Swap the pot" with other potted plants. These plants are removed from their pot and placed in the buried pot for as long as you decide. This may work for a special occasion, a wedding, or birthday of a family member. Onlookers will be very impressed and envious with your horticultural "flare".

"Swap the pot"

CHANGE CONTENTS OF
AN EMPTY BURIED POT

Final Thought

*"Don't tell your friends you have
gone potty."*

HOME-MADE PLANT LABELS

These are needed to identify your plants or identify where seeds, bulbs, or dormant perennials have been planted. Labels can be tied to a branch, or you can also place little discs of wood, chopsticks, or rocks with the plant's name on it.

My tips and tricks

- Make your labels out of discarded white plastic milk bottles cut into strips.

- Find small, smooth little rocks that can be painted with a plant's name and decorated as well, if desired. They last longer and allow your family to "rock" all day.

- Collect any tree branches that are at least seventy-five millimetres thick. These can be cut into "discs" approximately thirty millimetres thick, and can then become natural plant markers, once written upon.

- Keep disused plastic chopsticks for plant labels when marked with a permanent pen.

- Buy copper name tags available in nurseries and tie them onto the plant after you have indented the correct name on them.

Final Thought

"Tag me if you can."

ORCHID CARE

Most people struggle to get their orchids to perform enthusiastically each year. All plants need light to thrive, and if there is extra light, they will produce more flowers. Most people make the mistake and place their orchid plant (after it has flowered) in an area with little light, for example, under a lemon tree. To have better success with blooming, read on.

My tips and tricks

- Remove flowering stalks after the last bloom has opened, so the plant can start "planning" for next year.
- Place the plant in morning sun (in Australia) until Christmas, and then in filtered light until the new blooms begin to open.

- Don't repot the plant regularly, as it will flower better when the roots are slightly root bound.
- Feed the plant after it has flowered. Commercial orchid foods are good. You can use liquid fertiliser monthly or slow-release osmicated granules.
- If you have rainwater, then use it with orchids.

Final Thought

"The orchid is Mother Nature's masterpiece."

PERENNIALS

Perennials provide any garden with the opportunity to have year-round colour and excitement. Just visit the Chelsea Flower Show in London and witness the vast choice of plants that offer imaginative and beautiful plantings. Perennials can also offer waves of colour in a tiered manner, to help create the famous English cottage border.

In Australia, the intensity of colour may be less due to the strength of the sun, but the longer growing period in a temperate garden compensates for the subtle colour loss. In temperate climates, these plants grow wider, requiring more frequent division, more feeding, and more watering. The abundance of flowers from a perennial border "feminises" any garden and counterbalances the greenness of shrubs close by (when they are not in flower).

My tips and tricks

- Avoid buying "invasive" perennials that create more work.

- Deadhead flowers frequently, if you can, to encourage more flowering.

- Share your little treasures with friends and neighbours when you are dividing any perennial plants.

- Leave a marker in the ground to identify the spot where any of your perennials die back completely each winter, for example, Hostas (Hosta sp.).

Final Thought

"Come into my garden for the greatest show on earth. Admission is free."

CLIMBERS

Climbers, when grown on a wall, arbour, or trellis, can make any garden three-dimensional. They can be evergreen or deciduous, flowering, fruiting, or spectacular with autumn colour. Although these plants are traditionally grown as climbers, there are no rules that say you can't grow them as a ground cover or have them cascading over a wall.

My tips and tricks

- Create a support for a climber with the use of wires, staples, ties, welded wire panels, lattice, or sheets of concrete mesh for those stronger or heavier plants. Using mesh panels gives this type of support longevity. These panels can also be temporarily laid forward if the fence or wall needs repair or painting. Once the work is completed, the panels can be reattached to the wall. These large panels can also offer increased security for your property, when fitted above fence height.

- Cut out a small section in the middle of the creeper and place something ornamental or artistic "nestling" in it.

- Help climbers to get off the ground. When starting a self-clinging climber, for example, a climbing fig (Ficus pumila), use Blu-Tack or tape to start the self-clinging process. Then, cut off any floppy bits to encourage vertical growth only. You will be surprised by the outcome with this little bit of effort.

- Trim your climbers as needed and remove any ground growth, for example, from ivy (Hedera sp.).

- Be creative and combine two climbers together, for example, a blue and a white wisteria (Wisteria sinensis), or try a climbing Lorraine Lee rose on an arbour with a white clematis (Clematis sp.). Your friends will be looking for your third green thumb with envy.

- Create style by plaiting (braiding) a wisteria plant (Wisteria sinensis), or create a diamond pattern with Star jasmine (Trachelospermum jasminoides).

Final Thought

"Just stick with me."

TRELLIS AND LATTICE

Trellis is usually made of treated pine panels, but some gardeners may make their own out of bamboo canes or long cuttings after pruning. Lattice can look attractive when framed, but it can be expensive to buy and erect. Its use should be limited as it deteriorates over time. This is because creepers rapidly distort and break the panels and the small, galvanised staples that hold them together don't last long, as they start to rust. Sometimes the weight of the climber, especially after rain, can easily break the panels.

There are synthetic panels now available to overcome these issues, and they can add style to your boundary fence line.

My tips and tricks

- Think about the above issues before you buy.

- Check whether your fence or brick wall is sound enough to hold the weight of a lattice screen.

- Weigh up the cost of purchase and instalment against any other benefits.

Final Thought

"So, lettuce be smart."

ESPALIERS

The technique of layering a plant, usually fruit trees, allows more room in a picking garden. This technique encourages you to train the plant in a paired symmetric manner, initially supported by a strong wire frame or attached to a wall. Espaliers then allow any fruit to be picked more easily.

My tips and tricks

- When you espalier a plant, it creates great style. It then becomes a decorative feature to attract one's eye, especially when laden with ripe fruit. (For example, citrus plants are a beauty to look at when they bear fruit.)

- Become artistic when you paint the trunk and branches of a deciduous espalier with a vegetable dye. Its appearance in winter, against a brick wall, can be dramatic.

- Study the appropriate pruning techniques to maintain the symmetric look.

Final Thought

"Adam should have had his apple tree espaliered."

TUSSIE-MUSSIES

A tussie-mussie is a small posy of herbs and miniature flowers that are added to some foliage, preferably fragrant. These sentimental bouquets were more popular years ago, when given to friends and family.

You can vary the contents, but try to incorporate some fragrant cuttings from your garden.

There is nothing more exciting and beautiful than receiving a tussie-mussie.

My tips and tricks

- Realise you can make a tussie-mussie throughout the year.

- Check your garden, especially your herb garden, for appropriate fragrant cuttings to make a tussie-mussie.

- Make this ideal gift for your hostess when you are asked out for dinner, and experience the response.

- Plant any of the following long flowering plants (in temperate climates) to have almost year-round flowers, some examples being Geraniums (Geranium sp.), South African daisies (Osteospermum sp.), Blue daisy (Felicia amelloides), Mexican sage (Salvia mexicana), Florist's floss flower (Ageratum sp.), French lavender (Lavandula dentata), Seaside daisy (Erigeron karvinskianus), Fuchsia 'Tom Thumb' (Fuchsia sp.), Abelia (Abelia grandiflora), Sweet pea shrub (Polygala grandiflora), and Yellow marguerite (Euryops pectinatus).

- If you have an excess of small, fragrant flowers and leaves, consider making potpourri. Here, petals and leaves are dried in the oven on a baking dish until they are dry but not brittle, and then sprayed with a favourite essential oil. The material is placed in a perforated bowl and its fragrance can last up to two years. Some examples include roses, lavender, mint, thyme, basil and marigolds for colour.

> *"Flowers always make people better, happier, and more helpful. They are sunshine, food and medicine for the soul."*
>
> —Luther Burbank

Final Thought

"When you give, give yourself."

GROWING TREES
IN LAWN

You often see grass growing happily at the base of a tree in a park, and yet struggle to achieve the same result at home. Lack of water combined with cutting the grass too short compounds the grass's survival rate as it attempts to compete with the tree's horizontal feeding roots.

My tips and tricks

- Leave at least a 1.5-metre circle around a tree when you plant it in the lawn. Your new tree will grow much faster without the competition from the grass. Once the tree is at its desired height, you can let the grass grow back.

- Keep the grass under the canopy of a tree greater than thirty millimetres, especially in the warmer months.

- Feed and water the lawn near the trees more frequently, to compensate for the competition from the trees.

- When planting new trees, use a piece of PVC or conduit as a stake. You can now fill these "tubular" stakes frequently with water and watch your young tree grow more quickly.

- Many suburban gardens in Australia have super large gum trees (Eucalyptus sp.) growing happily, with all the nutrients and moisture a city garden has to offer. The excess of trees in suburbia followed a trend forty years ago to only plant indigenous (native) gardens. These trees regularly drop branches and limbs, especially after a storm. These make the trees undesirable due to the danger they create, especially to children playing close by. Best not to plant any more eucalypts in suburban gardens.

- White trunked birch trees (for example, Betula pendula) always look great growing in a green lawn, especially in a group.

Final Thought

*"A society grows great when old men
plant trees whose shade they know
they will never see."*
(Greek proverb)

SECURITY WITH PLANTS

Some people believe that there is a money plant, often called the jade plant (Crassula ovata), that should be planted near your front door to create financial security. This section now refers to plants that only offer physical security (intruder proof) and will deter people entering one's property, especially those with thorns.

My tips and tricks

- Plant bougainvillea so it can sit atop a fence. Climbing roses can also be used. No one will penetrate a thorny bougainvillea that is offering you almost year-round spectacular colour in mild climates.

- Plant any thick, thorny shrubs, for example, the common hawthorn (Crataegus sp.) to achieve the same result. Other examples include Holly (Ilex aquifolium), Darwin's barberry (Berberis darwinii), and Pyracantha (Pyracantha 'Orange Glow').

- Plant very dense trees, for example, conifers or trees with thorns, to impede entry into your property. For example, False acacia (Robina pseudoacacia), Honey locust (Gleditsia triacanthos) or Lisbon lemon (Citrus x limon 'Lisbon') can also be very effective.

- Other climbers attached to tall sheets of concrete mesh will also impede intruders.

Final Thought

"Security problems are only opportunities with thorns attached to them."

CONTROLLING WHITE BUTTERFLY

All gardens benefit from the beauty of colourful butterflies as they go about their fluttering, attracted to colourful, bright flowers. Their bodies collect pollen to help fruits, vegetables, and flowers produce new seeds.

It is interesting that the plainest of butterflies, the white butterfly, can be such a pest in the vegetable garden. They produce ravenous green grubs that destroy the brassica family (cabbage, cauliflower, broccoli, Brussels sprouts, and kale).

My tips and tricks

- Cover any susceptible plants with fine netting to stop access of the white butterfly.

- Make a cocktail of 50 per cent plain flour and baking soda. When ready, spray it on, preferably on a cool day.

- Let your chooks run free, if you have any, and let them feast on the green caterpillars.

- Physically remove all green caterpillars (which are well camouflaged) if it is practical.

- Plant dill, sage, thyme, and mint to ward off white cabbage butterfly attacking your brassica seedlings.

Final Thought

*"Lettuce pray for our cabbages
(Cole Slaw)."*

REMOVING WHITE SCALE

Sometimes, the removal of scale can be difficult. Repeated sprays of white or pest oil at six-week intervals can help, but the dead scale insects take a long time to fall off. Stressed plants, especially those that are underwatered, seem more prone to scale attack than healthy plants. Soon, ants appear to feed off the nectar from the scale insect, and then sooty mould arrives soon after.

My tips and tricks

- Take control and only have healthy plants by providing proper feeding and watering schedules.
- Spray all scale with pest or white oil as needed and repeat, if necessary, every six weeks.
- Remove resistant white scale on old rose branches with a toothbrush dipped in pest oil. This method

not only kills the scale but physically removes it at the same time.

- If the problem is only affecting a few branches, just prune off the affected areas and discard.

Final Thought

"Don't take life too seriously, as you may not get out alive."
(Bugs Bunny)

FOUNTAINS

People seem to love a fountain. Just toss a coin into it and who knows what might happen. My landscape experience shows me that ponds and fountains are troublesome. If you want one, then read on.

My tips and tricks

- The pond should be at least twice the size of the height of the fountain to avoid any splash out. This splash out can make the surrounding paving slimy, slippery, and dangerous.

- Ensure the pond is at least forty centimetres deep, to allow water plants the chance to grow easily.

- Always buy the best quality pump. They last longer.

- Brighten up your fountain with quality underwater lights.

- Add a few fish (ideally, native varieties) to give children and grandchildren an interest. Get them to name each fish, for example, Bluey, Mr. Splash, Ginger Megs, and so on. Have some fish food on hand.

- Create a regular cleaning timetable for the pump, especially in the warmer months.

- Buy some water plants. If you have at least half of the water covered with foliage, the water will remain clear.

- Make sure your pond is childproof, by having a mesh panel placed approximately seven centimetres below the surface. This mesh screen can also prevent birds from eating the fish.

- Turn the fountain off on windy days to reduce water being blown away.

- A drop or two of vegetable oil left on the surface of your water feature will help reduce mosquitoes.

- Concrete cattle troughs come in different sizes that are perfectly round. They make perfect ponds for fountains. They are also much cheaper than trying to make a perfectly round pond at home.

Final Thought

"Keep your three coins until you visit Rome."

"CRAZY, CRAZY" PAVING

A concrete driveway or path looks unattractive when cracked or old. It is unlikely you will do anything about it, but if you want a creative and low budget outcome, then read on. Our landscaping team tried these techniques once and the result was amazing.

My tips and tricks

- Create a positive outcome in a cracked driveway when you make further cracks all over the area with a mini jackhammer. The area will now look like "crazy" paving. To dramatically improve the appearance, add a red brick header course laid on mortar. To add more pattern (with cross banding), cut out enough space to add the same bricks. You can also add black oxide into the cracks. You now have an old-world look that may suit your style of house.

- For large, old concrete areas that look shabby, hire a concrete cutter and superficially cut the area into equal square areas (approximately four hundred square millimetres). The area will now resemble a paved area. You can now paint alternate squares with a mixture of black oxide mixed with boncrete (a waterproof additive). The checkerboard appearance is worth the effort.

Anecdote

I once worked on a landscape site that had marble crazy paving. What was interesting was that the marble was sourced from all the broken pieces that are normally thrown out. They were all different sizes and colours and laid in between brass metal strips, for the perfect end result.

Final Thought

"Even the smallest achievements pave a way to great success."

—Mary Kay Ash

GRAVEL DRIVEWAYS

Gravel driveways are not liked by all, especially when young children like kicking the gravel about. But they are a great option for the budget conscious, especially for people with very long driveways. Maybe you have noticed large garden estates in the UK that have long gravel driveways arriving at the forecourt that dreams are made of.

Other bonuses of a gravel driveway include the pleasing "crunchy" sound as you walk on it, and the benefits of easy ground access if future services are to be added to the garden (for example, electronic gates or garden lighting). A gravel driveway also allows rainwater to penetrate the ground, instead of it entering the storm water system and being lost to the general garden. To lower the water bills for the garden and have a gravel driveway or path looking its best, follow the advice below.

My tips and tricks

- Prepare the base with at least ten centimetres of crushed rock that is then compacted, so that it is firm.

- Plan a slight gradient, so that there is good drainage without excess water pooling.

- Cover the base with your selected gravel or pebbles to a thickness of thirty millimetres only. Any thicker, and it will show tyre or wheelbarrow marks and will also cost that much more.

- Buy a proper gravel rake, so that twigs and leaves are raked up, leaving gravel behind. A normal leaf rake never does the job correctly as it gathers too much gravel mixed with the leaves and twigs. So, the tines (spikes) of the rake should be pointy.

- Remove any weeds by hand that have grown in the gravel, or use boiling hot water on them as a weedicide.

- Always leaf rake in the direction of a breeze, to make it easier.

- At home, I rarely need to gravel rake my driveway more than once a month, whilst enjoying this passive exercise.

- Remember, the crunchy sound can discourage a potential intruder.

Final Thought

"My favourite road I've been on ain't paved."

—Viktor Tatarczuk

STOPPING INVASIVE PLANTS

Invasive plants are harmful to our natural resources because they disrupt natural forest structures, waterways, and ecological processes. In our homes, invasive plants can smother other plants and their roots can cause damage. Weeding around these plants is almost impossible.

My tips and tricks

- Keep the problematic plant (for example, culinary mint), in a buried container to restrict its root run. The base of the buried pot can also be cut out.

- Place root barriers in the soil to reduce any spread of roots. These can be bought at large hardware stores or made from old vinyl floor coverings. Just cut them into lengths that are forty-five centimetres in width. Dig a deep trench and place the barrier in it, so it sits vertically, and then backfill.

- Don't buy any of the problematic plants in the first place, as they can create a lot of work.

- Keep informed about invasive plants by regularly checking with your local council. Plants that were once accepted for the home garden (for example, agapanthus and some pittosporums) are now considered to be "weeds" by local councils and now can't be sold in nurseries.

Final Thought

"These species are not inherently bad, they are just in the wrong place."

CUTTINGS TO GENERATE NEW PLANTS

Plant cuttings offer greater uniformity (clones) of your plants whilst rewarding the home gardener with the excitement of producing new plants.

Ideally, only take cuttings from healthy plants and preferably in the mornings, when it is cooler. Friends, neighbours, and family always treasure them, as they know you chose a special plant to strike. So, "strike" the first blow and create new plants for someone's garden.

My tips and tricks

- Always cut the top of a stem cutting horizontally, and the bottom obliquely. This informs you which end goes into the propagating mix. The increased surface area of the oblique cut assists in establishing more roots very quickly for a new plant. This technique is crucial when taking grapevine cuttings.

- Remember that stem cuttings produce new roots whilst root cuttings produce new stems.

- Always use a quality propagating mix.

- Rooting powder or rooting liquid can be bought in nurseries. The cutting is dipped into it, and any excess is then flicked off, as excess causes root distortion. Honey can also be used as a rooting medium.

- Create the holes when planting the cuttings with a disused chopstick.

- Create a mini greenhouse to house your cuttings, and keep the moisture and heat in by using the right size clear plastic sheets or bags.

- For aerial cuttings, surround the "wound" that is made on a branch with sphagnum moss and wrap it with plastic kitchen wrap.

- Other shrub cuttings can be made by layering a low, long branch covered with soil. Roots appear and you now have a new plant.

- Share your new plants. Friends and neighbours will never forget this kind gesture.

Final Thought

*"Every plant has their own
requirements in order to grow, and
so do people."*

HERBS

We are all familiar with the benefits of eating and cooking with herbs, especially in recent times. Migrants have added new flavours to what was, years ago, our very bland food.

I grow just a few herbs such as rosemary, thyme, chives, and flat-leaf parsley to add to different dishes.

My tips and tricks

- Plant the herbs you like anywhere you like. They don't all have to be in the vegetable garden.

- Pick leaves by hand and tougher stems with secateurs.

- Shape your herb plant as needed.

- Don't overfeed them as this may reduce their fragrance.

- Cut small bunches of herbs to give as a personal gift when you are asked out for dinner, or add them to a posy.

- Buy a cookbook that highlights the use of herbs, to herb your enthusiasm.

Final Thought

"Gardens need time and gardeners need thyme."

HOSES

Hoses were first made in Australia by Dunlop in 1908. Go to any large hardware store now and witness the wide range and quality of available hoses to buy. They come in different colours, lengths, and sizes to meet our needs.

My tips and tricks

- Always buy the best quality.

- Make sure you buy the right length, that will reach all plants.

- Avoid leaving the hose in full sun where it will eventually become damaged, and stop running your car over it, as it will split.

- Water fights with a hose or bucket are fun. Don't forget to "scream" when the kids get you.

- Store your hose safely to prevent accidents.

Final Thought

*"Hard-to-reach plants don't like
short hoses."*

WATERING CANS

People find watering their little treasures with a watering can to be very therapeutic. Fortunately, larger watering cans have markings (up to nine litres on their side), which allows accurate doses of fertiliser to be added to water.

My tips and tricks

- Buy two watering cans, one for general use and the other for chemical use. Don't forget to mark them appropriately.

- Buy some little coloured watering cans for your children or grandchildren. Get them to write their names on one.

Final Thought

"Let us grow strong roots, watering and nurturing each other daily."

—Sanjo Jendayi

GARDENING TOOLS

Double ended tools are not sold anywhere, but no one ever said you are not allowed to use both ends of your tools.

Fortunately, very few tools are needed to complete the majority of tasks in a garden. A leaf rake, a hoe, and a spade are the three basic ones. Leaving excess tools lying around results in more being lost and also creates the dangers of them being left outside overnight.

My tips and tricks

- Buy quality and preferably long handled tools (a shovel versus a spade) to help reduce back strain.

- Use the handle end of a shovel to help compact soil in a large pot instead of your fingers. For smaller pots, use the handle of a trowel. For tiny potted plants, for example bonsai and cacti, use the end of a pencil or disused chopstick to compress the soil. Once again, NEVER USE YOUR FINGERS TO COMPRESS ANY SOIL IN ANY POT unless you are wearing quality gloves.

"Hooray for
double ended tools"

- Use the tip of the handle of your hoe to flick out stones or small pieces of paper caught at the base of a plant.

- Use the handle end of your hoe along a garden bed, to create an even edge as you drag it along.

- Help move heavy objects by keeping any old handles from your tools and then using them as "rollers" to shift heavy items.

- You can use a strong shovel handle intelligently as a crow bar, but be realistic and be careful not to break its handle.

- Create a small hole in the ground with the end of your shovel to plant bulbs or seedlings, just like a long-handled dibber.

- Mark the handle of your shovel with a measuring tape so you can have measurements readily available as you garden. These can assist with the correct placement of plants or for measuring anything that needs it.

- Paint part of your tool handles yellow, so they are easier to find at the end of the day.

- Clean tools after use, and wipe them with engine oil (except the handle, of course), especially over winter, to prevent them from rusting.

- When using any tool, always think of your and others' safety by storing your tools carefully.

- Record the number of tools entering the garden at the beginning of the day and later that day, the number of tools brought back in. A good habit is to leave each tool on or near a path after using it, so it is easily seen for further use or available to pick up at the end of the day. To leave any tool in the garden overnight is unacceptable, but this often happens. Preventing accidents should be everyone's highest priority.

- Keep small gardening hand tools and ties in an old disused letterbox attached to a post, in your vegetable garden, for easy access.

- Buy a trigger spray nozzle for your hose to minimise water wastage.

- To avoid losing your secateurs, buy a leather holster, so that your secateurs are readily available. You will never regret buying one.

- Don't go "golfing", but garden instead. Just carry a few long-handled garden tools in your old golf bag as you work around your garden. "Provisionals" are not allowed.

- Keep the worn-out plastic head of your leaf rake. When you have two, remove the handles and then use the two plastic heads as "giant hands" to pick up large piles of leaves.

- Use pegs to "seal" your gloves after use, so bugs don't get inside.

- Reuse old rake handles that are in good condition as a perfect stake for a large container. The rounded top makes the stake look classier.

- Use an old wooden pallet, standing vertically, to store your long-handled tools.

Final Thought

"If you can't be the sharpest tool in the shed you can always be a garden hoe, as a dirty hoe is a happy hoe."

WHEELBARROW USAGE

Although the use of a wheelbarrow appears to be straightforward, its incorrect use can be dangerous and tiring.

My tips and tricks

- Grip the handle ten centimetres from its end, where it enlarges. This will help with stability, especially over rough ground.

- For safety, push your barrow in preference to pulling it.

- Place more of the load above the wheel, for much easier movement.

- When emptying the barrow, tip it into the selected spot and pull back the barrow sharply by its legs. This action quickens the emptying. It is more effective than holding the handles, and swaying the barrow from side to side as if you are "dancing" with it. At the end of a day of barrowing, you won't be as tired.

- Some wheelbarrows won't die, and they can finish up as flower containers. A sad ending. If I was a wheelbarrow, I'd prefer to go to parties as an "ice bucket" holding cold drinks.

- Always store your wheelbarrow vertically against a fence or in the shed.

"Roll out the barrow and have a barrow of fun"

Final Thought

*"Roll out the barrow, for we are going
to have a barrow of fun."*

ARTISTIC OUTCOMES AND OPPORTUNITIES IN THE GARDEN

There are many ways of creating focal artistic spots in your garden, especially with recycled materials which usually finish up at the tip.

My tips and tricks

- An old sheet of corrugated iron can be cut into geometric shapes for a tree mobile. You can also cut out animal and bird shapes to be placed in the garden.

- Quirky signage on small pieces of corrugated iron or flat pieces of old wood can be a bit of fun as well. For example, "Have gone gardening".

- Turn old, rustic pieces of timber to frame a mirror or a trompe l'oeil (an optical illusion) to hang on a wall.

- Collect old paint tins or terracotta pots of different sizes to be painted different colours, to form a selection of herb pots.

- Collect different shaped leaves, flowers, twigs, and small stones to create macrame with your children and grandchildren.

- Use old pieces of welded mesh to hang tools on.

- Keep cuttings from a grapevine to make a wreath for Christmas and spray it red for a great effect.

- Paint alternate fence palings different bright colours around a children's play area.

- Paint the trunks of trees with vegetable dyes mixed with Parasoline (a white powder used to cool down glasshouses). The effect is dramatic, especially if the trees form a copse or when there is a magnificent specimen tree on the long axis of the garden. When painted, it looks like a piece of sculpture. French blue is my favourite colour. Obviously, the dye fades with time, but the effect remains.

- Cut up small branches of wood (into the same length) from any tree that you prune. When wired together, they can be made into small rustic fence panels for the vegetable garden. Long greener branches that can be bent easily can be woven into panels as well.

- Roll disused barbwire into a large ball, as large as you can, if you have enough of it lying around. Ideally, the ball should be one metre in diameter for maximum effect. Then, place it safely in your garden as a piece of sculpture. Add a low solar panel ground light close by, for night-time enhancement.

- Make a quality cover for a re-sited clothesline. This creates a dining or seating area in your garden under your new "umbrella".

- Reuse any old flat sheets of welded wire mesh and turn it into a compost bin, shaped as a cylinder.

- Create interesting animal shapes, for example, a chook or duck, out of disused chicken wire and place them in your vegetable garden.

- Reuse any lengths of bamboo for an "ornamental piece" in a small Japanese garden. Five bamboo poles of varying lengths can be tied together as a bundle with thick black rope, which can be attached to a brick wall that has been painted black or red.

- Reuse old pieces of timber to make a "safe" tree house. It does not have to be high. A few old tyres can create a small, secretive entrance.

- Let your plants become "famous". Create topiary, plait small plants, for example, Ficus (Ficus hillii), Bay trees (Laurus nobilis), lengths of Ivy (Hedera sp.). Start when plants are young and plait their supple branches together.

- Other plants can develop new identities when braided or grown on frames in a diamond pattern. Large and small wire frames of animals can be bought or made, and "filled out" with your favourite creeper, for example, the Maidenhair vine (Muehlenbeckia complexa). These animals can be grouped together for further interest.

- Triangular flat wire frames, the shape of a Christmas tree, can be placed vertically in a special pot and covered with a creeper.

- Crochet "sleeves" can be made to cover branches of a small tree near your patio area, using different colours and patterns. Sounds a little extreme, but you now have your own home-made live artistic "ornament". Obviously, you use old, leftover yarn. The end result is exciting.

- Finally, if you can find a paperbark tree (Melaleuca sp.), remove a sheet of bark and write a poem on it. Children can also have great fun using pieces of bark to make novel gift cards or paint their pet.

<u>*Anecdote*</u>

I once saw a group of topiary animals with an elephant three metres tall standing on a lawn, as if they were grazing on it.

Also, an artistic gardener in Evandale, Tasmania, would grow plaited tomatoes and petunias each summer in a pot. Quirky, but fascinating.

Final Thought

"Recycling is more fun than riding a bike."

HAVING FAMILY FUN IN THE GARDEN

Many gardeners have no fun in their garden, and that is a pity. They see gardening as repetitious, getting dirty and tired. Other gardeners embrace the garden as a friend that provides awareness and inner peace. For them, gardening is another day at the "plant".

So, if gardening gets tough, the tough look at ways to increase the amount of fun they can have at home, outside.

My tips and tricks

- Continue all ball games and other sporty activities as a family, as children enjoy these activities whilst getting a good dose of Vitamin D.

- Start a new family game not played before. For example, Bocce, where eight large metal balls are cast at a smaller wooden ball. Teams can have two or four balls each. A great family game that can be played on the lawn or a gravel path.

- Swimming pools enable families to have lots of fun in the garden.

- Trampolines, if you can afford one, allow action and develop physical skills.

- Being outside has the additional benefits of exercise and distracts children away from their phones and online games.

- Build a pizza oven and find out how many new friends you now have.

- Create a firepit for lively family discussions. Have the marshmallows close by. Keep a garden hose on standby, just in case.

- Camp overnight with your kids under the stars. I'm sure there is "tent service" available overnight, just as there would be "room service" if they slept inside. You can also have breakfast outside as well.

"Have fun in your garden"

SLEEP IN A TENT OVERNIGHT WITH YOUR KIDS

- Let the kids lie on a beach towel in their sandpit and plan their next beach holiday with you.

- Set up a movie night outside on the deck with lollies, popcorn, and ice cream readily available.

- Create a special dining event with candles, streamers, and balloons, even if you bring the dining room furniture outside.

- BBQ something different, for example, eggplant slices coated with olive oil.

- Wheelbarrow rides around the garden still create excitement and fun, especially when you go faster and run through a water sprinkler.

- Have a good old fashioned water fight if none of the above appeals to you.

Anecdote

A kid was asked what he wanted to be as an adult. The answer was "a bigger kid".

So, have fun in your garden.

Final Thought

"It is more fun when you're not the only one having it."

(The Oaqui)

MY IDEAS FOR
A JAPANESE GARDEN

Japanese gardens are rich in symbolism, philosophy, and religion. Many plants in our gardens originated in Japan and were collected by those brave seamen, travelling along the tea and opium trade routes. Japanese gardens exhibit a natural and often minimalist look at the relationship between plants, water, rocks, pebbles, and sand, which are all placed with extreme care. A small courtyard garden may consist only of a single large rock, strategically placed like a sculpture and surrounded by raked sand. A larger Japanese garden may show a mountain scene, with cascading water over rocks, and dense plantings with delicate foliaged trees promising autumn colours, for example, Japanese maples (Acer sp.). Japanese gardens can also be exciting in spring with spectacular splendour when the flowering cherry trees (Prunus sp.) are in full bloom.

My tips and tricks

- Choose plants that are preferably of Japanese origin.

- Select plants that have interesting features to create a visual focus. For example, a tree that has a "distorted" trunk, or a weeping tree that does not stand straight but slopes away, as if the wind has blown it sideways. Place an interesting rock next to its trunk, so that the rock looks like it is stopping the plant from falling over.

- Paving, especially the zigzag variety made of flat slabs of stone, offers more interest than the straight variety.

- Select trees that have a light canopy and can allow filtered sunlight through, as if the sunlight is going to bless the garden.

- Make different structures out of different sized bamboo poles, for example, screens and small fences.

- A few bamboo poles can be tied together with thick black or red rope and then attached to a wall as an artistic feature.

- Add water features such as ponds or cascades, as they add great interest.

- Authentic Japanese deer scarer water fountains (Shishi-odoshi) are made from a piece of bamboo that is pivoted. As the bamboo fills with water, it falls over and its end hits a rock and then the cycle is repeated.

- Create a traditional "lowered" dining area, where you are seated on the ground near a low table or with your feet placed in a "pit". This creates a "focal" and authentic place to eat, relax, and even roll over onto cushions and have a snooze, when desired.

Final Thought

"Create a garden where less is more."

MY IDEAS FOR A SHADY GARDEN

Shady gardens are very challenging as they are usually under large trees, where there is restricted light and competitive tree roots. Yet there are many ways to create something special, such as a long bench, with appropriate plant selection or some ornamentation. Even a day bed could be strategically placed for use on warmer days or maybe a double sized hammock swinging from branches above.

You may realise that plants in full sun have 100 per cent light and grow readily. In partial shade, there is at least 50 per cent light and many plants are happily placed there. In full shade, plants may have less than 50 per cent light, and therefore, plant selection is imperative for vitality when growing in the shade.

My tips and tricks

- Choose the right plants. For example, Natal lily (Clivia nobilis), Spur flower (Plectranthus ecklonii), Forest bell bush (Mackaya bella), Cast iron plant (Aspidistra elatior), Begonia hybrids, Impatiens hybrids, assorted ferns, especially the small varieties (Asparagus setaceus), Glossy leaf paper plant (Fatsia aralia), Gold dust plant (Aucuba japonica), and some indoor plants.

  It is interesting that the Clivia plant (Clivia nobilis) is rarely mentioned on lists of shady plants. Yet, in my experience, it is the most spectacular and successful shady plant with minimal maintenance requirements.

- Reduce the competition of tree roots on smaller plants. Dig a large hole, where you can, between any large tree roots. Place a 43-centimetre plastic pot in the hole at ground level and fill it with enriched soil. Plant your favourite coloured specimen in this "walled" mini garden and you will be surprised with the outcome. Neighbours will swap their green thumbs to know how you did it.

- Remember the "swap the pot" idea mentioned earlier.

- Compost the area heavily to help maintain moisture, and at the same time, to provide more nutrients.

- Find and place an interesting piece of sculpture or a comfortable bench under a tree.

Final Thought

"Watch these shady characters take control."

MY IDEAS FOR
A MYSTERY GARDEN

No one ever said that a garden has to be formal, regular or boring. Mystery gardens create excitement and a sense of fun, especially for children.

My tips and tricks

- Create "connecting" compartments in your garden with the use of clipped hedges, short and tall.

- Create a winding path that gets narrower. At the end of the path, step behind a clipped hedge, shrub or tree into the next garden "room".

- Release unusual sounds through your speakers, for example, hooting owls.

- Create a trompe l'oeil, a "trick of the eye" as a focal point.

- Hang distant, quirky signs to attract your eye, for example, "Free range children", "Come and take control".

- Place an attractive old door (with its architrave attached) onto a brick wall or back fence. Then, leave it fractionally open to stimulate the inquisitive mind.

Final Thought

"Come and meet my head mystery gardener."

(Sherlock Gnomes)

MY IDEAS FOR
A CHILDREN'S GARDEN

There is something very wholesome when children or grandchildren are interested in the garden, especially the vegetable garden.

The whole garden is like a classroom for them, where different leaf shapes, fragrant plants, and flowering habits can be pointed out. At the same time, a garden offers opportunities to have lots of fun.

My tips and tricks

- Think "safety" as the number one priority in a children's garden. I must say it again: think "safety" as the number one priority.

- Let children or grandchildren select a spot in the vegetable garden that they think is "theirs". Ask them to make and place a sign with their birth name on it, where it can easily be seen.

- Long, slender leaves found in the garden can be placed on the lawn with a number on them on windy days. Then watch as they "race" each other, as the wind blows them around. No gambling, of course.

- Buy some seeds and seedlings that you know will be successful, and then have fun planting them. The children will experience the journey plants take from seeds or small cuttings. Enjoy the pleasure of completing these tasks together. At the end of the day, there is great satisfaction in knowing that your knowledge and experience is being passed on.

- Get them to plant some colourful annuals, such as pansies or lobelia, which last such a long time.

- Pick "their" vegetables together when ready, and get them to include those vegetables in the evening meal.

- Encourage them to decorate their area with gnomes, fairies, or ornamental animals.

- Large pieces of bark can have drawings done on them.

- Make a little "house" out of large cardboard boxes, with cut-out windows and a door. Let the kids decorate it, and impress them with lunch supplied. You will be amazed at the excitement they will get from "building" their own cardboard house.

- Supply small, colourful gardening tools, watering cans, and floral gloves.

- Teach them how to make their own home-made liquid fertiliser.

- Get children to make their own plant watering bottle, from a large plastic drink bottle whose lid has been drilled.

- Buy or make a worm farm, covering an area of approximately sixty square centimetres that's twenty centimetres deep. Five hundred grams of worms will now consume half their weight each day (exclude any onions, citrus, or scraps of meat from your kitchen scraps). One cup of worm juice diluted in nine litres of water will get every plant moving. Remember, worm racing is not allowed. With Greta, we will have "Global Worming" sooner than later.

- Teach children how to make a "scarecrow" that will stand "guard" over their garden like a "babysitter".

- Keep playground equipment in a large and generous space. Then cover the ground underneath with special "playground only" woodchips, at least twenty centimetres deep, to create a softer and safer base.

- Cover any sandpits (yes, sandpits are still lots of fun) with a sheet of lattice to keep any animals out. This is preferable to plastic, which always blows away and frequently has snails, slugs, and small spiders living underneath. If the sand is a little wetter on any day, it won't interfere with children at play.

- Create a "fitness" area with ropes to swing from, some basic outdoor gym equipment, basketball hoops, dart boards without the spiky darts, and pool activities. Add some vigorous gardening to make the garden more appealing to be in.

- The old fashioned "mud kitchen" remains popular for toddlers. Old clothes paired with coloured plastic bowls and dishes work best. Eat their "meals" at your own risk. Ideally, wash those toddlers outside before their hot bath inside.

- Frisbees are still great fun in the garden.

- Egg and spoon races and sack races keep aerobic activity going, with determined would-be winners hard at it. Have a soft towel on hand to wipe those wet foreheads.

- Chalk can be used for drawing, hopscotch, and decorating.

- Build a home-made tepee for hours of fun.

- Enjoy their excitement when your grandchildren visit you and race off to see what's happening in "their" garden.

- A photo of them in "their" garden makes a great memento for them to take home.

- The old-fashioned car tyre on a rope is still appealing, with as many children aboard as possible.

- Treasure or Easter egg hunts have always been fun.

- Collecting interesting and uniquely shaped leaves or those with different sensory touch can be educational.

- Some children may be interested in "flower pressing", which can be stored in an old photo album.

- Feed native birds away from predators and have a water dish close by.

- Get children to decorate their own gumboots.

- Allow your children to develop community caring projects, with a "community box" that is preferably waterproof. It can be left at the front gate with excess vegetables and herbs or used books for others to have.

- A long sheet of plastic laid on a slope (if you have one) can become a "slippery slide". The screams of joy are louder, especially when some household detergent is sprinkled with water onto the plastic.

- Grow dramatic flowers, like sunflowers (Helianthus annuus).

- Reassure them that unruly children will not be used as weed pickers.

- The ultimate fun game is a water pistol or water gun "fight". This is the best "get the kids fit" activity, as they frantically chase each other around the garden. My advice to adults is to stay inside, as kids can run a lot faster than they can.

Final Thought

"Why try to explain miracles to your kids when you can just have them plant a garden."

—Robert Brault

MY IDEAS FOR
A FOLIAGE GARDEN

Foliage only gardens are best seen in forests, where different leaf shapes combine with coloured foliage. The ground is then blessed by filtered sunlight as the sun's rays penetrate the tree's canopy. Leaves can be needle shaped, elliptical, round, large or small, smooth edged, furry, serrated, and so on. Leaves can also range in colour from white to cream, light or dark green, gold, bronze, purple and red. Others can also be variegated, gold and green, or cream and light green.

Creating foliage gardens in the city adds an intense botanical character to any garden and a cooler space for contemplation.

My tips and tricks

- Plant a group of Japanese maples (Acer japonica) for a blaze of autumn colour. Another alternative is to plant a group of birch trees (Betula pendula, "Moss White") for their autumn foliage combined with the purest white trunks.

- A selection of small, interesting shrubs with variegated foliage, for example, Japanese Dwarf sacred bamboo (Nandina nana) or Gold dust plant (Aucuba japonica) can create an intense botanic look at the base of trees. Small shrubs with great leaf shapes, for example, the Oakleaf hydrangea (Hydrangea quercifolia) or the Japanese Aralia (Fatsia aralia) can also add strong foliage character. Finally, plants with architectural foliage (ferns) or needle shaped leaves create more opportunities.

- Create a space in your foliage garden to bring your mind to rest.

Final Thought

"I am not always green with envy."

MY IDEAS WHEN DESIGNING SMALL GARDENS OR COURTYARDS

These intimate spaces become more special when you realise that they look larger because they are three-dimensional. This characteristic becomes more obvious when they can be seen vertically, from a veranda or an upstairs room.

My tips and tricks

- Select plants with larger foliage in the foreground and much smaller foliage as you move further away.

- Use multiple mirrors for a dramatic enlargement of the space.

- Crazy paving can be laid with the pattern decreasing in size. Here, you lay larger slabs in the foreground and then lay slabs of decreasing size as you move away. This "optical illusion" creates depth in your small space.

- Paint the far wall sky blue, even with some birds flying by so that it looks like the sky, or paint a mural of distant farms and hills.

- Keep the area uncluttered by selecting smaller furniture and fewer pieces.

- Let the inside adjacent room spill out, especially if they are both on the same level, so both spaces feel as one.

- Vertical gardens on walls have a lot to offer in small spaces as no garden beds at ground level, which would erode ground space, are needed.

- Alternatively, create shelving, with your favourite small plants in colourful containers placed on them.

- Add fragrant plants to your selection. These grow well in a warmer, more stable environment of a courtyard, as the house acts like a "heat bank" to keep the courtyard's night temperature higher. This makes the small garden more inviting, planted with subtropical plants such as gardenias (Gardenia florida, which grows so well in Melbourne).

Final Thought

*"Little gardens great and small, often
are the best of all."*

MY IDEAS FOR FRAGRANT GARDENS

Although fragrant gardens may bring romance, I would recommend other more reliable sources. There is no doubt that women love fragrant plants more than men, with gardenias, daphne, and fragrant roses being the most popular.

"The greatest gift of a garden is to flirt with one of the five senses" (sight, hearing, taste, touch, and smell).

My tips and tricks

- Select fragrant plants for courtyards.

- Cut flowers from fragrant plants that can be enjoyed inside as well.

- Share these fragrant flowers, for example, a small posy, with intimate friends.

- Strip the flowers off branches from fragrant shrubs, for example, English lavender (Lavandula angustifolia) and dry them. Place small amounts into a sachet and hang it in a wardrobe. The same sachets can be placed near your kitchen rubbish bin to suppress any odours. The leftover fragrant branches can be used as skewers, for lamb shashliks on the BBQ.

Final Thought

"Who scent this fragrance to me?"
Perhaps it was Kalvin Kline.

MY IDEAS ABOUT SEASIDE GARDENS

The power of sea breezes, wind, turbulence, and tunnelling are a few of the challenges experienced in seaside gardens. Salt is not the issue that people believe it is. Just look at how well plants do in the sheltered rear gardens, close to the sea. Seaside plants exposed to a lot of wind must feel like they are growing in front of a "hair dryer" for hours on end, and they don't like it. Keep this issue in perspective, as any problems you may have with wind seem small against the dramatic bonus of a sea view.

My tips and tricks

- Choose plants that are stage 1 tolerant (when you have absolute beach frontage). Be careful with your selection, as plant lists often exaggerate a plant's happiness to live so close to the sea.

- Choose plants with thicker leaves as they do better than plants with thinner ones.

- Build screens from lattice or brush fencing to absorb the wind. Often old railway sleepers can be placed vertically, at different heights and spacings, for an effective and rustic wind-absorbing fence.

- Plants may need their own plastic wind guards, which act as a sleeve to protect them against the elements, especially when young.

- Cover beds with an abundance of mulch, to help retain moisture from prevailing winds.

- Plants in seaside gardens are happy to have a frequent "shower" from a hose, to wash any salt off.

- Choose seaside grass plants whose foliage always seems to be swaying backwards and forwards in a sea breeze, creating a very wavy and soothing look.

- Collect any seaweed off the beach, especially after a storm. Check your local council, as some discourage or disallow this activity. If you do get it home, spread it over your garden, as it is very rich with minerals. You don't need to wash it first.

- Try to find some "Vitamin Sea", as that is all you need to seize the day.

- Find some old seaside flotsam and jetsam (for example, driftwood), washed up fishing buoys, or lengths of thick marine rope to decorate your garden.

- Find the right spot for seating (preferably a bench) to enjoy the sea views and beautiful sunsets.

Final Thought

"Always have a shell in your pocket, sand in your shoes, and beach happy."

GENERAL INFORMATION FOR THE KEENEST GARDENER

If you are creating a new garden or renovating an established one, the process is the same. The outcome directly relates to the quality of the design and if you get the design right, most times you get the best outcome.

Good design relates to how each space (or room) is to be used, whether the room is inside or outside.

If you employ a qualified landscaper, garden designer, or landscape architect, they will need to have design skills, hard landscaping, and soft landscaping skills. Additional general knowledge of plants, planting, feeding, watering, pest control, and general maintenance skills will also be useful. Hopefully, they will have owned a garden at some stage of their life, so they can understand the emotional aspects of being a keen gardener.

Finally, understanding the different types of plants, their names, and meaning may be of interest to some gardeners, but not all.

WHAT ARE PLANTS?

It appears unnecessary to explain what plants are, until you ask someone to explain the difference between a tree and a large shrub, or the difference between an annual and a perennial. Nurseries don't help us, as they rarely display plants in their groups or have good signage to help confused customers. This general lack of clarity is the reason I have included this information in this book.

We know that plants are multicellular organisms with over 320,000 species and 16,167 genera. Unfortunately, they are rarely seen as our vital friends, committed to our well-being and survival.

My book offers my very simple definitions of plant groups. So, read on, and see if you agree with me.

Trees are the plants whose branches emerge from the top of a trunk. They may be small (under six metres), medium sized (under thirty metres), or tall (over thirty metres). They may be evergreen or deciduous, and have attractive foliage, flowers, fruit, fragrance, or bark. Their appearance may be round, columnar, oval, pyramidal, vase-shaped or weeping. They may have spectacular autumnal features or spring flower abundance. When planted in a group as a copse, they will have a more exciting appearance than if planted singularly.

Shrubs are the plants whose branches emerge from its base. Once again, they can be small (under one metre), medium sized (under three metres), or tall (over three metres). They can also have the other characteristics that trees have.

Annuals are the plants that complete their life cycle in one year and are usually grown for seasonal colour.

Biennials are the plants that complete their life cycle over two years.

Perennials are a very large group of plants that flower enthusiastically in waves of colour. There are three types of perennials that I recognise, yet most gardeners are only aware of the first variety.

The first group are "Herbaceous perennials" and they are the largest group of all. Many die back to a crown in the cooler months, especially in colder environments, while others will die back completely in the winter months, for example, Hostas (Hosta sp.). All of them re-emerge vigorously in spring.

The next group are the "Shrubby perennials", which have the appearance of a small shrub, but are distinguished by not having woody stems, for example, French lavender (Lavandula dentata) or geraniums (Geranium sp.).

The last group are the "Fleshy rooted perennials" that store a lot of moisture in their roots. They can happily grow in the sun, for example, Agapanthus (Agapanthus orientalis), or in extreme shade, for example, the Kaffir Lily (Clivia miniata).

Bulbs are really part of the perennial family.

Ferns are a group of plants, often with fine architectural foliage that grow well in moist, shady areas.

And yes, what is my definition of a "weed"?

Weeds are "unwanted" plants whose seeds wait patiently to germinate over many years. Some suburban councils now consider some plants as "weeds" and forbid nurseries to sell them. Some of the examples are Agapanthus (Agapanthus orientalis) and the Sweet pittosporum (Pittosporum undulatum). These two plants spread readily into local bushland and ultimately become expensive to remove.

Without vigilant control of weeds, "one year of weeds can become seven years of weeds".

Final Thought

"A weed is a plant that has mastered every survival skill, except for learning to grow in straight lines."

—Doug Larson

PLANT NAMES.
WHY BOTHER?

We can all remember meeting new people at a party and then struggling to remember their name shortly after, an embarrassing moment. For most people, trying to understand and remember a plant's name can have the same outcome.

So why would I include this topic in my book, if it is going to be so difficult? The reason is that in 1753, a Swede named Carl Linnaeus published a book, *Species Plantarum*, that created international agreement for plant names. This was the starting point for the naming of plants with agreement in every country. Ever since then, there has been an appreciation for the origin of plant names and their meaning. Understanding plant names may be useful, but it becomes unnecessarily confusing when everyone uses different names for the same plant. Gardening practitioners, TV hosts, garden magazines, garden books (except *Hortus Third*, the horticultural "bible") freely swap plant names around and around. Sometimes botanical names are used, but other times a plant's common name or nickname is used.

There is no consistency, and guess what? I am convinced that these matters won't change in the future.

Let us now look at all the plant names that exist, even though we don't use them all.

Family names: These are rarely used by home gardeners. For example, Iridaceae, the Iris family.

Generic names: These are frequently used. For example, Daphne. Generic names usually appear to be one of three types. They are of Latin or Greek origin, or sometimes, they are commemorative (that is, they are named after someone). These commemorative names often end in the letters "ia", and by removing these two letters, a person's surname is revealed. For example, a Magnolia, a Gardenia, and a Begonia would become Magnol, Garden, and Begon. These surnames may now tell us whether they are of Spanish, English, or French origin. If you also have knowledge of the discovery of the world by those brave sailors in the fifteenth, sixteenth, seventeenth, and eighteenth centuries, you may now realise that shipping routes of discovery, trade, collecting, and colonising involved many countries. There were English, French, Spanish, Portuguese, Americans, Russians, and Swedes. If you know which explorers went where, you may now know where each plant will be placed in your garden.

Species names: These are also frequently used. Species names appear to be of five types. They either describe the country of origin (for example, japonica means "of Japan" and sinensis means "of China"), habitat, habit, leaf or flowering characteristics, or once again, they can be commemorative and end in the letters "ii" or "ianum". For example, smithii becomes Smith and willmottianum becomes Willmott, and so on.

Common names: These are commonly used. For example, the Cigar plant for Cuphea ignea.

Cultivar names: This is a botanical name that is followed by an epithet (often a hybrid). For example, Grevillea banksii is a pure species, whilst Grevillea banksii "Ruby Red" is a cultivar and Grevillea "Superb" is a hybrid cultivar. These names are created by plant growers.

Nicknames: As with humans, nicknames are used very commonly in the plant world. They are often quirky, for example, the Norfolk Island hibiscus (Lagunaria patersonii) is called the Itchy Pod Tree by locals. A gorgeous viola (Viola tricolour) is sometimes called heart's ease because of its medicinal value, and other times called Johnny Jump Up (in the USA) or wild pansy (in the UK).

In this book, I have used common names first and the botanic name next, in brackets. The generic name's first letter is in upper case and the first letter of the species is in lower case.

If you need more information, then read *The Hillier Manual of Trees and Shrubs*, which has all of the practical knowledge you need to know about plant names, summed up in five pages.

So, let's get excited to see what the generic and species names really mean.

There are other names outside these classifications, for example, dulce means "sweetness" and praecox means "early". These names, and others similar to these, are very useful in describing plant characteristics.

So, when I first heard of the plant Wisteria sinensis, I knew that an Englishman named Wister (he was actually an American) collected this clambering climber in China. Because China was in the east, I would plant it facing east. Again, a plant called Sky flower (Plumbago capensis) would be planted in the open, as capensis means "of the cape", in South Africa. These observations are not totally reliable, but you will be surprised how often you can decide where to site your new plant, just by reading its label.

Another way of remembering plant names is to keep any plant labels for future reference, or just walking through a nursery, reading the labels of any plants you like, as I did many times.

Anecdote

I once met a fascinating lady who was selecting her seeds for her vegetable garden, whilst sitting in front of a log fire in the lounge of a ski resort hotel. What evolved was a discussion about plants having a spirit. She introduced me to the "Findhorn Movement" in Scotland, where its followers communicated with the conscious intelligence of nature and the plant kingdom. They understood the healing power of nature on the body, mind, and spirit. So, talking to a tree or large shrub may sound strange when it took place weeks before its re-sisting or major pruning.

The RHS did an experiment where ten tomato growers talked to their tomato plants. Interestingly, the tomato plants all grew taller with the talkative group than the control group.

Also, remember our grandmothers were communicating with nature as we often heard "mutterings" as they gardened. Did they have inside knowledge, you may ask?

Just don't talk to any garden gnomes or fairies.

Final Thought

"Just talk to your plants as they understand you."

ASSESSING
YOUR GARDEN

Pre site analysis information that might be available and useful.

If you have invited a consultant to your home, you will be surprised by the amount of general information he or she may have prior to knocking on your door.

For example:

- Your name (of course), sex, and possibly your age.

- Your address. Is the area residential, commercial, or other?

- The quality of other gardens and houses in the street.

- Any parking issues outside your property. Can a landscape vehicle and trailer fit into the spot? Are there any time restrictions or congested streets?

- Quality of the nature strip. Does it need repair or replacement?

- Is the garden sloping or are there any steps? These can seriously affect site access and raise any labour costs.

- Style of existing garden and condition of the existing plants. Are there any iconic plants to keep? Do any plants need removal, or are there any that could be re-sited into a more appropriate position?

- The size of the garden. This can be crudely calculated by counting the number of fence posts (usually placed at three-metre intervals) by the width of the property, which has been stepped out. Obviously, a tape measure will be used later, if you are invited to quote the job.

- Quality of paths and driveway. Are they damaged? Are they wide enough? Do they drain well?

- Do pets live there?

- Do children live there, where safety becomes such a priority?

- Are the owners keen gardeners or will their garden require future maintenance?

- Is there an obvious sprinkler system and is it damaged? Are there any obvious dry spots where the sprinkler system is not reaching, or any very damp spots where there is moss growing, indicating the system is leaking?

- Are there any simple handyman jobs needed, for example, missing fence palings, damaged down-pipes, dripping taps, weeds in the gutters, or damaged steps?

Any of the above observable features can not only impact on the design of a garden but can also affect the final budget. The above listed features will form part of the scope of work to be included in any brief and eventual quote. Nothing should be excluded, so a pen, paper, tape measure, camera, and shovel (to check the soil) should be available to properly assess any garden.

The initial meeting is best held with both partners present, as ideas from all concerned will need acceptance if you are to proceed.

So, when the consultant knocks on the door with all the information they have gathered so far, they should start by listening carefully to the owner's ideas and needs.

SITE ANALYSIS AND
PREPARATION OF A BRIEF

This is the most important part of creating your special garden, whether you do it yourself or a consultant does it for you. Don't forget the significance of the streetscape, as this is often overlooked when we only become involved with the issues inside the property.

Create a list of all negative features of the area you are assessing. The list may include any negative features in your borrowed landscape, for example, a neighbour's shed or clothesline, lack of shade, a sloping block, drainage issues, invasive plants (like oxalis, onion weed, bamboo, and ivy), etc. Garden beds may vary in size with mismatched plants as a result of previous owners' purchases, so these features also need to be recorded. You may notice a garden shed that is incorrectly placed. Fences may be in poor condition, and neighbours' trees may be causing problems. There may be a lack of privacy, small verandas with inadequate paved areas, or old swimming pools needing repair or replacement. Just keep adding to the list. Poor quality plants that have passed their amenity value may also be problematic and need removal. Check access to the property, as this may also be challenging, especially if machinery is needed.

It is critical to record a site's negative components in full.

You can now make a list of the garden's assets. Positive things to look for include a garden's generous size, its orientation to the sun, its functional use if flat, and any shade from trees. Are there any features in the borrowed landscape to be included (for example, a magnificent specimen tree in the distance, the volume of foliage neighbouring gardens offer free of charge at fence height, and perhaps a historic church spire)? By including the borrowed landscape, your space will appear larger. Try and keep any distinctive trees or shrubs on site, for example, a specimen or weeping tree, an old fruit tree or any tree that is quirky in shape. These may provide focal points to catch your eye or have spectacular flowering or fruiting characteristics in season. You can be loyal to great or older plants and include them in your design, whilst some designers only want a clear "canvas" before they start their design, thus devaluing existing assets.

Once recorded, these lists become part of the scope of work.

GARDEN DESIGN PRINCIPLES

Most people would be very happy with a garden that looks great in all seasons, is low in maintenance, and is reliable, whilst others are aware of the benefits of good design and want to know its process.

Garden design is similar to interior design, where spaces (or rooms) are designated by their proposed use. In a house, one room will be the dining room, another a bedroom or kitchen. Each room is designed accordingly. The process is the same outside as well. A front garden may be a large room with three functions: pedestrian, vehicular, and visual. A rear garden is usually a larger room, with multiple uses. It can have a recreational use (a pool or trampoline), a visual use, storage facilities, a cooking area, a dining area, or a relaxation area on a veranda with a day bed or hammock in the shade of a tree. Each rear garden will need an area for its services, for example, pool heaters and filters.

Identify the space to be designed

Start the design process by decluttering the site with the removal of broken furniture, pieces of unused timber, old bricks that have no use, and any other general rubbish lying around. Also, resolve any "structural" conflict that exists where there are a variety of fences or an assortment of hard surfaces, for example, concrete paths adjacent to brick paths alongside a bitumen driveway. The difference before and after decluttering any garden will be profound, as decluttering readily makes the space appear so much larger.

Garden design does not need to be complex. Just embrace the ideas given in the coming pages.

Final Thought

"There is a quiet peace to be found in the heart of a garden."

CHOOSE THE STYLE OF GARDEN YOU WANT

Is it to be a native or a picking garden, a Period, an Italian, or even a Japanese garden? You might want a formal garden, a coastal, or a wild garden. Often, the style of the garden relates to the style of the house, or its age. You decide.

<u>*Anecdote*</u>

I once designed a garden that had a religious theme, where all of the plants had biblical common names, for example, Solomon's seal (Polygonatum spp.), Monkshood (Aconitum sp.), Judas tree (Cercis sp.), Burning bush (Euonymus atro-purpurea), Star of Bethlehem (Ornithogalum umbellatum), and Jerusalem sage (Pulmonaria officinalis), to name a few. Of course, the owner was a minister of religion.

Final Thought

*"You don't need to follow trends
to be stylish."*

CREATE UNITY
IN THE GARDEN

Unity occurs when there is a harmonious relationship among all elements and characteristics of the design. Similar sized garden beds add unity, as do walls (fences) when they are similar in height and are made of the same building materials (timber, brush, or brick). Many gardens that I reviewed had a small wooden fence on one side, a larger one with rails on the other, a brick wall on the third boundary, and a painted rendered wall of the house which made up the fourth wall. This garden room then had "structural and visual conflict". This does not happen inside the home, where all the walls in a room are usually made of the same material and are all painted the same colour. Unity when planting can also happen, where you avoid planting "one of this and one of that".

Final Thought

*"A garden is a great teacher. It teaches
patience and careful
watchfulness; it teaches
industry and thrift; above all
it teaches entire trust."*

—Gertrude Jekyll

CREATE BALANCE
IN YOUR GARDEN

Balance is achieved when there is equalisation of visual weight from one part of the design to another. This can be achieved when the volume of foliage is similar in all beds (not tall, thin, deciduous trees in one bed and small evergreen shrubs in another).

As a garden has the ability to be three-dimensional, it will look special if you start by creating the tall garden, usually with trees planted six metres apart. You can now create the middle garden of shrubs up to three metres tall ("neighbours be gone"), planted 1.2 metres apart. This planting can screen any negativity from next door as well as creating a "living fence" to disguise unappealing fences. The base garden completes the planting, with a great variety of small shrubs, perennials, and annuals usually planted one metre apart. By looking at a garden this way, it reduces the common occurrence of a garden having a gap, almost like a missing tooth. The garden now offers foliage, flowers, fragrance, and seasonal variation at all levels.

Final Thought

"Live a life that has balance."

CREATE A FOCAL POINT (Axis Geometry) ON THE LONG AXIS AND CROSS AXIS

Once the spot is identified to catch your eye on the long axis of your garden, you can create a special planting (for example, a weeping tree), a bench, an urn, or any small structural object (for example, a gazebo or arbour). Sometimes, there is an opportunity to have two long axes, which can have the same feature and a cross axis as well. This opportunity ties the garden together, strengthening its unity and design.

Final Thought

"The human spirit likes a little bit of geometry."

MAKE SURE EVERY PART OF THE DESIGN IS TO SCALE

This design principle is often overlooked or not understood. Scale is best achieved by creating a pleasing proportion between one element and another. So, when you place a bench under a tree, and not a seat, then the seating is in scale. Similarly, a chosen urn on the long axis should not be too small.

Outdoor paved areas or decks should be in scale to meet modern outdoor living requirements. The deck should be generous in size, but not too big. If it is in scale, it will allow easy movement and enable larger outdoor furniture enough room. These areas will now be more appealing to use, with the bonus of them being safer at night.

Garden beds also need to be similar in size (not one half a metre wide and another four metres wide).

Final Thought

"Get off the scales and start gardening."

CREATE SEASONAL VARIATION

Most gardens are at their best in spring, but inspirational gardens have part of the garden at its best in each season, especially when there are three or five of the same plants creating united splendour. Whether it is a group of flowering plants or a group of small trees at their autumn best, the dramatic effect is the same. WOW!

My tips and tricks

- Few plants can offer a special effect in every season, but the ornamental pear trees (for example, Pyrus calleryana "Redspire") are an exception and are worth planting if you have the space.

- Seasonality can also be dramatic when a sea of bluebells (Scilla sp.) emerges in late winter at the base of a white trunked Silver birch tree (Betula pendula).

- Shirley Stackhouse's book, *My Gardening Year*, has lists of what is flowering each month, and gives us all the chance to select our favourites each season.

- Vegetable gardens are also seasonal gardens, offering fresh produce the whole year round. When they are picked in season, they are at their best, more abundant and often cheaper than in the stores.

Final Thought

"Let nature be in your yard."

—Greg Peterson

CREATE HARMONY
IN YOUR GARDEN

This happens when the quality of your garden matches the quality of your house, and is not related to marital bliss. Often, a very large house (or "palace") is built on a small block and has little outdoor space to match the personality of the house. Any free borrowed landscape will now be a bonus, especially if you can incorporate next door's plants as if they are in your property. By planting a flat "living screen" on your fence, for example, Star jasmine (Trachelospermum jasminoides), you can now "visually combine" your garden with the one next door and thus, make the space appear larger.

Final Thought

"Out of clutter, find simplicity."

—Albert Einstein

PUT YOUR SERVICE AREA IN "SPACE LEFTOVER"

The best place for sheds, clotheslines, storage, and equipment is down the side of the house in space leftover. This can create easier access for tools and equipment, for both the front and rear gardens. This service area can also address the concealment of rubbish bins whilst they are parked near a side door. The gardens of the sixties and seventies gave little regard to back garden aesthetics and often placed the garden shed or clothesline in the middle of the garden or on the long axis of the garden in complete view. Thankfully, we now plan our gardens, so we can maximise the size and functional aesthetics of the garden.

My tips and tricks

- The garden shed can be built in space leftover on the side of a house and can easily be made walk-through. A tidy shed is a safe shed.

- The clothesline can be fitted on a side wall of the house and will then benefit from air tunnelling through. It can be folded down when not in use.

- Pool equipment placed down the side of the house will be quieter and also cheaper to install, as it will be closer to the household's electricity supply.

- Herbs may fit happily in pots down the side of the house, where they will be more available to pick.

- Excess children's play equipment can be hung on the fence or house wall or on the shelves, if they fit.

- A garden tap placed close by would also be very useful.

- These areas are hard to landscape, especially if a plain fence is opposite a window. The view looking out is poor, so try a creeper growing on the fence, perhaps with an ornamental plaque or interesting art piece to catch your eye. If there is enough room, plant a sasanqua camellia (Camellia sasanqua) to offer seasonal flowers. This plant can be espaliered to maintain space.

Final Thought

*"Does every man need a shed?
Yes, and yes!"*

CONTROL THE IMPACT
OF TIME

When designing gardens or maintaining them, the concept of time is paramount, as we all know that "time flies". Time can then have different meanings, so read on and see how time impacts a garden or a gardener.

My tips and tricks

- Firstly, how much time does a homeowner have to maintain their garden? It is pointless creating a high-energy garden if the owner is time-poor. The garden will soon deteriorate, especially if they can't afford a maintenance gardener.

- Secondly, older gardens change with time, when small plants grow larger than expected. Plants initially planted in full sun may finish up struggling in the shadows, as trees grow wider. As plants themselves grow larger, they can become stressed when their roots now have to compete for moisture and nutrients with other plants close by. This can be minimised if all plants are placed at the correct spacing in the beginning.

- Thirdly, the longevity of a garden varies. Some plants live for many years (sometimes for over one hundred years), whilst others for only a few years (the pioneer plants). So, time can create "gaps" in a garden as plants pass their amenity value and are removed or as they simply die.

- Finally, time affects the growing pattern of plants in warmer climates. For example, perennials growing in Melbourne have a much longer growing season than those growing in cooler climates. This means they will require more feeding and watering, and will need to be divided up more frequently, increasing their maintenance (time) requirements.

Anecdote

I like the story of a ninety-eight-year-old man planting some acorns in his garden. He then goes inside to check out catalogues for a hammock. I guess he lives for tomorrow.

Final Thought

"All gardens and gardeners need thyme. Thyme for fun, thyme for rest, and thyme for themselves."

"Gardens and gardeners, all need thyme"

LIGHT UP
YOUR GARDEN

Garden lights are often overdone, where your garden looks like a runway at the airport. But other times, simple lights can give a garden its own mood and make a garden safer at night.

My tips and tricks

- All types of lighting have to be safe.

- Ideally, have one light (with a dimmer, even if it is low voltage), on the long axis of your garden, focussing on a specific feature. This may be a ground light shining upwards.

- Mood lighting (these can be solar lights) can outline your paved area or veranda.

- Ideally, have different lights on different switches, to avoid the "one or all" look.

- Pool lighting adds safety at night, especially if children are present.

- The only other lights I like, may be attached to your eaves, along paths, or near the garage or steps to offer safety at night.

- Make sure all electrical works are done by a qualified electrician and that there are no cables running along fence lines. All wiring should be in conduit, at least sixty centimetres underground.

- Never have extension leads running over the garden or clambering up an arbour or pergola. Unaware children or gardeners may be vulnerable to electrocution when they decide to do some casual pruning.

- Solar lights are safe and offer a great alternative at a much cheaper price.

- "Romantic" lighting (with the use of candles) is very special, especially when dining. The more the merrier, especially if they're large. Don't forget to blow them out when you leave the area.

- Coloured lights are a personal choice.

Final Thought

"To shine your brightest light is to be who you truly are."

—Roy T. Bennett

"So, give light and people will find the way."

—Ella Baker

LET YOUR EARS ENJOY VARIOUS SOUNDS

This may mean the crunching sound of a gravel path, wind whistling through the trees, rain falling on a tin roof, or the sounds of children at play. Sound may also come from cleverly placed speakers, bringing your favourite music, sounds of the ocean, or a favourite bird call.

My tips and tricks

- You will never regret placing speakers in your garden, especially on decks or verandas.

- Contrary to popular belief, noise is not totally reduced by planting shrubs, but only by solid walls or mounds, if you have space.

- Wind chimes are popular with most gardeners and best kept away from a neighbour's fence line.
- Perhaps you need a pair of hummingbirds, one male, the other female, to maintain their harmony.

Final Thought

"Sounds good to me."

HEAT UP YOUR INNER GARDEN

Heating in the garden is a more recent addition, as people now enjoy the outdoors at night.

My tips and tricks

- Heating may come from fixed overhead appliances, powered by gas or electricity.

- Other heaters are free standing and are often powered by gas cylinders and are usually mobile.

- More creative heating comes in the form of large iron bowls, chimineas, or braziers, which can be placed in a conversation "pit" for exciting discussions outdoors.

- Cook in them or on them, or just enjoy the occasional marshmallow on a stick.

<u>*Anecdote*</u>

I recently made a brazier out of a stainless steel washing machine bowl. It is a spectacular sight at night when a fire is lit inside and glows through the pores of the bowl. Buy one at the local tip for around six dollars.

Final Thought

"When I feel the heat, I see the light."

—Everett Dirksen

CONTROL SHADY OPPORTUNITIES

It is very difficult to use a garden without shade.

My tips and tricks

- When buying a house, be influenced by one that has shade trees in the rear garden.

- Plan your outdoor dining and relaxation areas in the shadow of trees, preferably trees that have a light canopy.

- Plant a tree immediately if you don't have any. Unfortunately, "the best time to plant a tree was twenty years ago".

- Erect sails or structures (for example, pergolas and gazebos) to achieve some shade.

- Don't ask any shady characters over, especially if they like to drink a lot.

Final Thought

"Gardens are not made by sitting in the shade."

—Rudyard Kipling

PRIVATISE YOUR SPACE

Most of us have queried our privacy in our gardens at times, especially our pool gardens.

Structural answers with screens, pergolas, and sails can resolve any lack of privacy, and they can be very expensive, but sometimes necessary.

My tips and tricks

- The best way to resolve the problem is to plant what will become a "living screen" from a large choice of taller shrubs. These can be clipped to three or four metres in height to keep their compactness whilst blocking out your neighbour. Smaller plants can be planted at the base of the screen to make it appear more natural.

- Taller growing trees may offer some screening, but they eventually lose their ability to screen when they grow too tall.

- In larger gardens, mounds offer some privacy and noise reduction.

Final Thought

"Neighbours be gone."

(This is the nickname of a screening shrub sold in Australia that grows quickly. It is one of the Lilly Pillies (Acmena smithii).)

UNDERSTANDING WIND

Many people do not enjoy wind. This can come in the form of a breeze, as wind (mild to severe), turbulence, and tunnelling (which occurs when wind rushes down the side of a building, or worse, when it tunnels down between two adjacent buildings).

A slight sea breeze on a hot day is welcoming, as is the sound of a strong breeze rustling through the trees. Severe wind can make the garden uninviting, and at the same time, dangerous, as tree limbs and house parts can be thrown about. Most plants, but not all, do not cope when planted in this "hair blower" environment, especially the plants with thinner leaves. A plant's shape can also become distorted as it tries to cope with severe wind.

Many people believe that it is the salt in the air that does the damage to windy stage 1 coastal gardens (those that have absolute beach frontage), even though the plants on the sheltered side of the house appear to do well. But it is invariably the persistent wind. How would we look and feel living in a windy environment each day? The answer is unprintable.

My tips and tricks

- You can resolve these wind issues when "Mother Nature" challenges us, with structures such as lattice screens, brush fencing, or nicely fitted sails and shade cloth.

- Plants such as compact shrubs like New Zealand Christmas bush (Metrosideros thomasii), Mirror bush (Coprosma robusta), and Boobialla (Myoporum insulare) can offer a more natural way of resolving these issues. They can be clipped tightly to make them wind absorbing living screens. Taller plants (mostly trees) can also assist in absorbing wind. Examples include Coast banksias (Banksia integrifolia), Norfolk Island hibiscus (Lagunaria patersonii), and the most majestic Norfolk Island pine (Araucaria heterophylla).

- Good garden design allows the wind to pass through a property or be absorbed, in preference to it confronting solid structures such as brick fences, and then causing turbulence and tunnelling.

Final Thought

*"Best to just keep the wind in
your sails."*

STRUCTURES
IN THE GARDEN

There are many structures that can be added to a garden, although most are expensive. Garden rooms, verandas, pergolas, arbours, pools, children's play equipment, and decks are the most common options. With decks, my experience says, "the bigger the better".

My tips and tricks

- You will never regret building a larger deck, especially if you do a lot of entertaining. If it is timber, it is smarter to stain it in preference to painting it. If left natural, a deck develops a more rustic look.

- Sometimes, structures can have more than one function, for example, a day bed on a patio can also have storage built inside.

- A structure may become more interesting when you add one or more mirrors to it, especially if they are framed with rustic old timber.

- Lighting added to any structure in the garden creates a special night effect.

Final Thought

"All good art is abstract in its structure."

PAVING OPPORTUNITIES

Creating hard surfaces in your garden can increase the opportunity to entertain on a firm, clean surface in preference to a lawn, with more desire to use this area at night. For a lot of people, aesthetics is the only parameter of choice when selecting which material to use. Yet, suitability, reliability, durability, and availability should also influence their choice.

The range of hard surfaces is vast, ranging from pebble or sand paths, tiles, concrete pavers, bitumen, stone, concrete, pebble mix, and timber. Sometimes, two materials can be combined to create a more interesting outcome.

My tips and tricks

- Paving designs vary, but the modern approach is to steer away from mono paving (where only one material is used), to paving that has some pattern, combining two materials at the same time. Pattern can be easily added to larger areas of mono paving when it is framed with a header course of bricks or pebble mix. Increased pattern can occur with cross banding as well, when using the same material as the header course.

- Remember that lighter coloured paving may be more attractive, but shows marks and grime more readily, whilst darker choices may make the paved area too hot to walk on in summer. So, be analytical with your choice.

- My choice is to use bricks, because of their durability and the ability to create patterns that combine well with other materials, for example, pebbles.

- All paving should have a slight slope to assist with drainage.

- The choice to seal your paving or not depends on which material is chosen.

- Gurney washing remains the best method to clean your paving in preference to an acid (hydrochloric) wash.

Final Thought

"If you don't like the road you're walking, start paving another one."

—Dolly Parton

We have now arrived at the end of the design stage, where decisions need to be made. Will you keep it simple and move forward with the DIY approach or involve professionals?

If the design process is overwhelming and you like the DIY approach, then do something simple. Lay out your garden hose aesthetically on your lawn, to create the bed shape and size you like. Now, one side of the hose represents the new beds, and the other side represents the lawn. Plant the beds out, feed and water your plants in, and then mulch. WOW! This will be finished by lunchtime, with a beer in your hand and a feeling of great achievement.

In contrast, if you choose professional help, your garden may look like a bomb site for a short time, awaiting the planned results. You decide which way you want to go.

I definitely recommend professional help, because at the end of the day, they will create something special and add value to your property.

Once the design has been accepted, the following stages occur:

The hard landscaping stage

This covers all the landscape works prior to planting. These include any demolition, excavation works, paving, concreting, structural changes, drainage, rockeries, retaining walls, pools, spas, steps, fences, screens, and the installation of sprinkler systems, speakers, and lights.

To complete this stage, a good landscaper needs some carpentry skills, brick laying skills, paving skills, and rendering skills, as well as many horticultural skills. All plumbing and electrical works need to be completed by registered tradesmen.

Soft landscaping stage

The placement of plants, planting, any staking, feeding, watering, and mulching now occurs. The garden should look "crisp" at the end of this stage, with beds not looking lumpy or overfilled, and plants placed with their best side facing forwards. This suggestion may sound petty, until you see a new garden where time has been taken to find a plant's best side, versus a garden where the plants are just placed in the hole, any which way.

This phase also includes a proper clean-up of the site, nature strip, and gutter at the end of works. Never leave any drinks, food, or personal rubbish on site if you want a future recommendation.

The consolidation stage

This stage follows an agreement between the landscaper and client to keep a closer eye on the garden for a period of three to six months. I highly recommend this inclusion in any contract signed, as it protects the client's investment.

Maintenance thereafter

The homeowners have to decide whether they will maintain their own garden or leave the garden to look after itself. The choice to hire a maintenance gardener will relate to your available time and your financial situation. Most average-sized gardens will need, on average, four to six hours of maintenance each week. So, if you miss one week of commitment, guess what is going to happen to your garden?

LET THE "GARDENING GAMES" BEGIN!

My ten favourite tips and tricks

- Use boiling hot water to kill weeds.

- Scrape your fingernails over a bar of soap before you start gardening, so that they are easier to clean later that day.

- Put an extra compost bin in the front garden, behind a large shrub. This will save you a lot of time carting vegetative matter to the back garden and bringing back the mulch months later.

- Make your own home-made "vegetable soup" out of vegetable peelings and scraps (which are commonly thrown out). When the "soup" is cool, feed it to your "friends" in the garden.

- Remove resistant white scale on roses with an old toothbrush dipped in pest oil.

- Always wash your vegetables outside in a perforated plastic basket placed in the garden. This reduces the water wastage, as this method does not see water going down the sink.

- Select plants for your garden that have at least three of the 5Fs (Foliage, Flowers, Fragrance, Fruit, and Freedom from disease).

- Select a cardboard box that is the right height when you are trimming small hedges. Just push the box along the ground with your foot as you clip the hedge to box height. If you are very clever, you can even land most of the clippings in the box.

- Experience the joy of giving fresh fruit and vegetables, or a small bouquet of flowers and herbs to a family member, a friend, or a neighbour, especially if they are in need.

- And finally, always WASH YOUR HANDS when you come inside.

Final Thought

"These ten favourites are easier to follow than the Ten Commandments."

CONCLUSION

The book is now available to all gardeners, old and new. By nurturing your garden, you are really nurturing yourself, with Mother Nature at your side.

Final Thought

"Old gardeners never die; they just spade away or vegetate, and then throw in the trowel."

—Herbert Prochnow
(In fact, if there are no gardens in heaven, then I'm not going.)

My Final Thoughts

To all my gardening friends,

What a re-leaf it is to finish my book, and I hope thistle cheer you up, as I carrot a lot about you.

I have been thinking about how to start my final message to you, so let me firstly say Aloe from my tulips. Please now accept my final words of advice on "The Wisdom of Gardening", from my head "to ma toes".

If you work away from home, always be happy with your celery. Don't let life serve you a lemon and never be melon cauli. Don't be a has bean, a runner bean, or a green bean that just strings along. Grow peas of mind, listen to sage advice, sow seeds of kindness, squash selfishness, plant smiles, and grow laughter. Make thyme for your loved ones and turnip to help your neighbours when they are in need.

Talk to your corn, as they also have ears, and watch your potatoes grow as they also have eyes. Don't converse with a hoarse radish and listen carefully when beanstalk. Don't give into pear pressure, sprout up when you can, and don't beet yourself up when something goes wrong, as this will affect your heart beet. Just bee the best you can be and orange your affairs accordingly, so you can always be "unbeetable" and thus, let your dreams be parsley met.

Ban Anna from the garden if she smokes her weed, and split from her. The rest of you should promise to be berry good, all the time. As there is not mushroom left, lettuce all be thankful, spring into spring when it comes, learn how to ginger along your garden path, and turn off your tap so there are no leeks. And remember that gardening is by trowel and error.

At the end of your day, squeeze your limes for a cool drink and ask Corey and a friend, Basil, for dinner. Also include Brussel Sprout for dinner, as he is a fun gi. He will entertain all at the table, so that there will never be a dill moment. Then you can eat, drink, and all be rosemary.

If your friends cantaloupe, then lettuce let them marry. Work out if Bok can bring Choy next time.

Later, jive with your chives, tango after eating a mango, and rocket all night. Then give Manda ring, to check if you really have to go to bed so early, as great gardeners have spent their whole day in their beds and you should be allowed to stay up all night.

Finally, just practice what you peach, be the apple of someone's eye, and try and be one in a melon.

Yours faithfully,

Okra Comfrey

You will never ever know if you never ever grow.

"Garden as though you will forever."

—Thomas Moore

With every donation, a voice will be given to
the creativity that lies within the hearts of
our children living with diverse challenges.

By making this difference, children that may
not have been given the opportunity to have their
Heart Heard will have the freedom to create
beautiful works of art and musical creations.

Donate by visiting

HeartstobeHeard.com

We thank you.

www.ingramcontent.com/pod-product-compliance
Lightning Source LLC
Chambersburg PA
CBHW051436050726
47593CB00005B/1805